A DETOUR TO
JANNAH

*"Even the longest road leads to His
mercy"*

Hajer Jemai

A Detour to Jannah

ISBN: 978-0-646-71291-8 Imprint: Hajer Jemai
Cover design by: Author
Printed in Australia First Edition

Disclaimer: The information in this book is for educational purposes only and should not be considered professional advice. The author and publisher are not responsible for any consequences resulting from the application of the information provided.

In the Name of Allah, the Most Gracious, the Most Merciful All praise is due to Allah, whose mercy knows no bounds, whose guidance illuminates the darkest paths, and whose love embraces even the most wayward of hearts. By His infinite grace, this book has come to life, and it is only through His help that every word has found its place. To Allah belongs all thanks and gratitude—for every moment of inspiration, lesson learned through trials, and an ounce of strength granted in times of doubt. Al-Hadi, the Ultimate Guide, calls His servants back to Him no matter how far they may have strayed. He is Ar-Rahman, whose mercy exceeds our shortcomings, and Ar-Rahim, whose compassion never fails. If there is any goodness in these pages, it is from Him alone. If there are any errors, they are mine. May He accept this effort, purify my intentions, and make it a source of benefit for all who read it. And may He allow it to draw hearts closer to Him, for He is the Most Generous, the Most Forgiving. Ameen.

A Note of Inspiration

This book was not written in isolation; it is the result of years of learning, reflection, and inspiration drawn from those who have illuminated the path before me. There were times when I felt lost when my heart was heavy with questions and uncertainties. But in those moments, Allah, in His mercy, always guided me to the right words, teachers, and reminders. Books became my refuge, my silent mentors, helping me navigate life's storms with renewed faith. Don't Be Sad and You Can Be the Happiest Woman in the World by Dr. 'Aid Al Qarni taught me the power of gratitude and resilience. Reflecting on the Names of Allah by Jinan Yousef deepened my understanding of who Allah is and how He is always nearby. Allah Loves... by Dr. Omar Suleiman reminded me of the beautiful qualities Allah loves in us. Timeless Seeds of Advice by B.B. Abdulla and Purification of the Soul by Jamaal Al-Din M. Zarabozo gave me gems of wisdom I often turned to in moments of doubt.

Beyond books, I was blessed to learn from incredible teachers and content creators who made the teachings of Islam feel deeply personal and relevant. My dear Ustadha Dalya Ayoub instilled in me a love for seeking knowledge and applying it daily. The powerful storytelling of The Digital Sisterhood podcast connected me to the struggles and triumphs of Muslim women worldwide. Soul Food offered spiritual nourishment in bite-sized reflections, and Sheikh Belal Assaad, Mufti Menk, Youssra Kandil, Dr. Haifaa Younis and Dr. Omar Suleiman's teachings resonated with me in ways that reignited my faith time and time again.

So many more voices, lessons, and moments of divine guidance have shaped this book—far too many to name. But I am deeply grateful to every person, author, teacher, and reminder who helped me along this journey.

May this book, in turn, serve as a source of light for those who need it, just as these works and individuals have been for me.

Alhamdulillah, always.

Contents

A Detour to Jannah

THE SCENIC ROUTE TO JANNAH

In the Quran, Allah reminds us that life is a test—a journey with valleys and peaks. Sometimes, we take the scenic route, wandering through detours that challenge our faith. But every winding path still leads back to Him.

You were born to parents who prayed for you before you were even in their arms. They whispered du'as, asking Allah to make you righteous, successful, and blessed. As a child, you looked up to them, hanging onto every word like it was the ultimate truth. You wanted to make them proud—and you did—until life began to shift.

Schoolyards replaced living rooms. Friendships bloomed, laughter echoed, and dreams stretched beyond the horizon. You grew taller, bolder, and convinced you'd outgrown the simplicity of childhood faith. By high school, hormones roared like tempests, reshaping your face, feelings, and worldview. Your parents' wisdom suddenly felt outdated.

"Why can't I go to the city at night?"

"You don't understand what it's like to be me!"

1

You asked these questions not for answers but out of frustration. Then, one day, a friend suggested something that seemed harmless:

"Tell your parents you're coming to my house, and we'll just go out from there."

It didn't feel like a big deal. Your parents were just being unreasonable anyway, right? And so, you took the first step—not just away from their rules, but from the values they taught you. What started as a minor detour felt harmless at the time. Little did you know how far it could take you...

Now, you have a part-time job and a university education. *"The world is your oyster,"* they say. You thought you had it all figured out. The freedom was intoxicating, and the variety of people, ideas, and cultures felt like a buffet you could sample from at will.

Each day, as you stood before the mirror, you adjusted your hijab, voice, and presence, hoping to blend in seamlessly with those around you. But every change and shift felt like you were moving further away from the person you truly were.

At first, it was easy to justify the changes. You told yourself it was temporary until you found your place. But as days turned into months, the weight of your choices became harder to ignore. Each glance in the mirror felt like a reminder that you were becoming someone you no longer recognised.

One evening, under the sterile glow of the bathroom light, your hand froze mid-motion. The eyeliner, the loosened hijab, and the practiced smile felt like costumes. And then, a question pierced your heart:

"Is this who I was meant to be?"

But even in that moment of doubt, there was a flicker of hope—a whisper from your soul reminding you of who you are and belong to.

Allah says in the Quran:

> *"And whoever fears Allah—He will make for*
> *him a way out." (Surah At-Talaq 65:2)*

Life's journey is rarely a straight line. Sometimes, we take the scenic route— winding roads that lead us through valleys of doubt and mountains of struggle. But even on the longest detours, Allah's guidance is our compass, and His mercy is our destination.

My dear reader, the fact that you hold this book—that your soul still whispers for truth—is no accident. That longing is Allah's **Rahma**, His divine rope pulling you back. You may feel unworthy, tangled in shame or regret, but listen closely:

Allah says:

> *"Say, 'O My servants who have transgressed*

3

> *against themselves, do not despair of the*
> *mercy of Allah. Indeed, Allah forgives all*
> *sins. He is the Forgiving, the Merciful.'"*
> *(Surah Az-Zumar 39:53)*

And the Prophet peace be upon him promised:

> *".....If you come to Allah walking, He will*
>
> *come to you running." (Sahih Muslim*
>
> *Hadith 2675)*

SubhanAllah! He isn't just waiting—He's running toward you. Your missteps, your stumbles, your ache to return? They're proof your heart still beats for Him.

Reflecting on that Ayah and hadith fills me with an overwhelming sense of peace and awe. We are human, and humans make mistakes—detours are part of the journey. But how blessed are we to have a Lord who is always ready to forgive, guide, and welcome us back with mercy beyond measure?

No matter where you are in your journey, know this: **the door to His mercy is never closed.**

What This Book Offers You

In **Part 1, Recognising the Detour**, we will explore the signs that reveal when the straight path feels out of reach—moments of emptiness, guilt, or a lack of purpose. Through reflective exercises and stories from the Quran and hadith, you'll see how being "lost" is not in vain but can be a turning point for spiritual growth.

In **Part 2, Reorienting the Heart**, we will explore the first steps of returning to Allah—beginning with repentance (**tawbah**). Through Quranic verses and stories of hope, we will reflect on how Allah's mercy is boundless and always within reach. We'll also address overcoming shame and guilt, reminding you that no sin is too great for Allah to forgive.

In **Part 3, The Journey Back**, you will find practical strategies for clearing the path to faith by detaching from harmful habits and influences. As we rebuild your connection with Allah through acts of worship, we'll discuss how to stay grounded in a world that constantly challenges your beliefs.

In **Part 4, Transforming the Detour into a Blessing**, you'll learn how struggles can strengthen your faith. Through gratitude, remembrance (**dhikr**), and cultivating the right company, you will discover how to surround yourself with practices and people that nurture your journey back.

Finally, in **Part 5, Walking Steadily Toward Jannah**, we will focus on maintaining consistency in faith, facing future challenges with resilience, and walking confidently toward the ultimate destination: Jannah.

A Detour to Jannah

Why I Wrote This Book

I always believed life was about moving. Keep going, keep pushing, keep achieving. Study hard. Work harder. Raise your children with love and patience. Don't stop, don't slow down, don't fall behind.

I prided myself on being capable, handling everything, and getting things done, no matter how exhausted I was. I had dreams, responsibilities, and a vision for my life, and I was willing to endure whatever it took to make it all happen.

But then, life handed me something I never saw coming—a chronic illness that ripped the illusion of control from my hands.
At first, I fought against it with everything in me. I refused to accept the pain, the exhaustion, the way it stole my energy and forced me to pause. I resented the way my body betrayed me, the way my plans crumbled, the way my life— once so structured—became unpredictable.

"Why me?" I whispered in frustration.
"Why now? Why this?"

I begged Allah for relief. I begged Him to give me back the strength I had always relied on. But no matter how much I pleaded, the pain remained. The exhaustion deepened. And the more I struggled against it, the more it felt like I was drowning in something I couldn't escape.

A Detour to Jannah

And then, in the stillness of my suffering, something unexpected happened.

I had to stop.

And in that stopping, I had to confront something I had been running from for so long—my heart.

I had spent years moving so fast that I didn't realise how far I had drifted from Allah. I still prayed, believed, and held onto my faith, but it had become routine and distant, something I did without genuinely feeling. Once soft and full of connection, my heart had become numb beneath the weight of my endless to-do lists.

I had spent so much time trying to be *everything* for everyone else that I had forgotten the One who had always been there for *me*.

It was a painful realisation. One that shook me to my core.

And yet, as I sat in the depths of my weakness, I realised something beautiful—something that filled my heart with both sorrow and relief:

Allah had never left me. I was the one who had drifted. But even in my distance, He had guided me back all along.

Through the stillness.

Through the suffering.

Through the very pain I had begged Him to remove.

And I knew I wasn't alone.

So many of us are fighting silent battles. Whether it's illness, heartbreak, doubt, loneliness, or simply feeling lost in the chaos of life—so many of us carry wounds that no one else sees. So many of us feel like we've wandered too far, fallen too hard, failed too many times.

That's when this book was born.

I wrote this for the ones who feel disconnected from their faith but don't know how to return. For the ones who pray but feel nothing. For the ones who carry guilt like a heavy chain around their hearts, convinced they are unworthy of Allah's love.

I wrote this to tell you that **your struggles do not define you.**

Allah's door is always open, no matter how far you've wandered, how many times you've stumbled, or how distant you feel.

This book is not here to lecture, shame, or overwhelm you with impossible expectations. It's here to remind you of something your heart may have forgotten:

You are never too far gone. The road back to Allah is always open. And He is waiting for you with more mercy than you can imagine.

May Allah soften your heart and illuminate

A Detour to Jannah

> *your path as you turn these pages. May He*
> *turn every detour into a bridge back to Him.*
> *And may your journey—however winding—*
> *lead you home. Ameen.*

PART ONE: RECOGNISING THE DETOUR

CHAPTER ONE
WHEN THE STRAIGHT PATH FEELS OUT OF REACH

Imagine standing at the edge of a forest. You know the path home is somewhere ahead, but the trees loom tall, the shadows stretch long, and every direction feels equally uncertain. This is what spiritual disconnection often feels like—a quiet, creeping sense that the road you're on no longer leads to peace.

Allah says in the Quran:

> *"And whoever turns away from My remembrance – indeed, he will have a depressed life…" (Surah Ta-Ha 20:124).*

But how did you end up here? How does the path that once felt so clear—the salah you prayed with focus, the Quran you recited with joy—fade into a fog of distractions and doubt?

Why The Path Feels Lost?

We live in an age of paradoxes: *connected but lonely, informed but confused, free but enslaved.* The very systems designed to make life "easier" often pull us further from the simplicity of faith. Let's walk through this maze together—not to condemn the world, but to understand how its traps ensnare even the sincerest hearts.

"You do you" Culture: In an age where individuality is celebrated as the ultimate virtue, we're sold a seductive lie: that identity is a blank canvas, waiting to be splashed with whatever colours we pluck from the digital aisles of TikTok gurus, Netflix narratives, and pop psychology podcasts. The mantra "You Do You" echoes like a liberation chant—a promise that empowerment lies in curating a self as fluid as a Spotify playlist. Swipe left, swipe right; mix and match beliefs like fast fashion. Want to be a Stoic minimalist by morning, a mystical astrology enthusiast by night? The world applauds your "authenticity." Yet beneath this glittering façade of choice, a quieter truth festers, we've traded depth for dopamine, coherence for clicks, and soulfulness for algorithms.

Our patchwork ideologies are stitched together with the fraying thread of convenience. TikTok serves bite-sized enlightenment between dance trends— "Five steps to manifest your best life!"—while Netflix reduces moral complexity to bingeable plot arcs, where heroes and villains wear designer hoodies. Pop psychology peddles empowerment as a product, shrink-wrapping ancient wisdom into Instagram mantras. The result? A generation clutching a collage of half-truths, mistaking aesthetic cohesion for actual conviction. We assemble identities like mood boards yet wonder why the glue of meaning doesn't hold.

This endless buffet of "options" is spiritual junk food—colourful, addictive, devoid of nourishment.

We scroll through a thousand lives, a million opinions, yet our souls starve. The paradox of choice becomes a prison: the more we customise, the more we homogenise. Algorithms herd us into echo chambers disguised as empowerment, where "doing you" often means performing a self-engineered for likes.

Freedom morphs into fatigue. We float in a sea of possibilities, unmoored from the anchors of tradition, community, or shared purpose—left to drift between the shallow shores of trend cycles.

Historically, meaning was a collective endeavour, a tapestry woven across generations. Now, we're handed scissors and told to cut our own cloth. But can a mosaic of soundbites sustain us when storms come? When grief, doubt, or existential dread creeps in, viral affirmations crumble like ash. The loneliness of self-authored belief systems yawns wide—a chasm no Netflix cliffhanger can fill.

This isn't a rejection of autonomy but a reckoning with its limits. "You Do You" culture, for all its rebellion against dogma, forgets that humans thrive in freedom and belonging. We're story-seeking creatures, hungry for narratives thicker than a Twitter thread and rituals

A Detour to Jannah

deeper than a #SelfCareSunday post. Spiritual malnourishment isn't a failure of individual will—it's the cost of conflating consumption with transcendence.

The buffet is open 24/7, but the soul, it seems, craves a feast we've forgotten how to cook.

The Prophet peace be upon him warned us about this saying:

> *"You will follow the ways of those before you, handspan by handspan, cubit by cubit—even if they entered a lizard's hole, you would follow." (Sahih al-Bukhari, Hadith 7320).*

Today, that "lizard's hole" is the algorithm—tailored to lead us further from the truth.

The Crisis of Khushu in the Digital Age:

Allah's question strikes like a thunderclap in the silence we've forgotten:

> *"Has the time not come for those who have believed that their hearts should become humbly submissive at the remembrance of Allah and what has come down of the truth?" (Surah Al- Hadid 57:16).*

But when was the last time your heart *truly* trembled? Not the performative piety of a folded prayer mat posted online, nor the fleeting guilt of skipping Fajr between snooze buttons—but the raw, uncurated submission that once cracked the voices of the righteous? Today, our hearts are not softened by dhikr; they are hardened by the dopamine drip of endless scrolling. Khushu—the stillness of a soul anchored in divine presence—has become a relic, drowned out by the cacophony of notifications. Our worship is fractured: one eye on the Quran, the other on the WhatsApp group buzzing with memes.

We live in an economy of attention where every app is a mosque competing for your salah. Anger is curated into clickbait headlines, fear amplified into viral conspiracies, and outrage packaged as "activism" to keep us doomscrolling. The Prophet peace be upon him warned against the *"hardness of the heart,"* but how could it not calcify when we feed it a diet of hot takes and comparison traps? We've replaced the sweetness of Tahajjud with the sugar rush of likes, mistaking the glow of screens for the warmth of Iman.

We pray as if checking tasks off a to-do list, then wonder why our duas feel like echoes in a hollow chamber.

The Brotherhood of the Algorithm

Consider the brother who shares a Quranic verse in his Instagram story— *"Whoever fears Allah, He will make a way out for him..."* (65:2)—and then spends the next hour refreshing metrics, tallying views like a merchant counting

15

coins. The verse, meant to dissolve worldly anxiety, becomes a trophy for social capital.

Brotherhood is reduced to follower counts, and empathy has been flattened into emoji reactions. We've digitised the ummah but lost the *umm*—the mothering essence of communal care. The man who once walked miles to visit a sick companion now sends a "Get Well Soon" GIF and calls it sincerity.

Allah names this sickness *Ghaflah*—the heedlessness that corrodes the soul:

> *"And do not be like those who forgot Allah,*
> *so He made them forget*
> *themselves…" (Surah Al-Hashr 59:19).*

Ghaflah begins innocently: *"I'll just check one reel."* But the algorithm knows your weakness better than your mother. It feeds you carousel posts on patience while hijacking yours, sermon clips about gratitude while stoking your discontent. Each scroll pulls you further from your fitrah—the primordial echo of *La ilaha illallah* buried beneath layers of digital sediment. You forget Allah in increments: a missed prayer for a meeting, a skipped verse for a viral thread, until one day you wake up a stranger to your own soul.

The Arithmetic of Emptiness

We are the generation that reads Surah Ad-Duha on our

phones but forgets to let its solace seep into our bones. We demand "authenticity" from influencers yet settle for fragmented attention in our salah. The Quran's question— *Has the time not come?* —is not an accusation but a mercy, a lifeline thrown into the storm of our distraction.

Khushu is not a mystic's luxury but the believer's birthright. To reclaim it, we must wage jihad against the colonisation of our consciousness. Limit the apps that hijack your hijrah. Let your heart *break* again at the Qur'an's truth. Weep, if only a single tear, before the King of Kings—He does not tally your followers, only your sincerity.

The choice is stark: We either unplug to reconnect, or risk becoming the ones who forgot, until even our shadows flee our hollowed-out husks.

"Hustle Culture" vs. Soul Care:
Allah's decree pierces through the noise of our endless striving:

> *"And I did not create the jinn and mankind except to worship Me" (Surah Adh-Dhariyat 51:56).*

Yet modernity has recast this divine imperative into a spreadsheet. Our worth, we're told, is a formula—degrees earned, promotions secured, side hustles monetised.

Worship is reduced to a bullet point on a LinkedIn profile, beneath "skills" and above "hobbies." We bow not to the Most Merciful, but to the cult of *productivity*—a deity whose altars are standing desks and whose hymns are podcasts preaching "rise and grind."

The Treadmill of More

Imagine the student who swaps Fajr for flashcards, whispering, "I'll pray later"—as if time is a vending machine dispensing second chances. Her compromise is not a single missed prayer, but a slow unravelling. With each dawn sacrificed to the god of academic validation, her soul's ledger slips deeper into deficit. She aces her exams but forgets how to weep in Sujood. Her heart, once a vessel for Quranic reflection, becomes a cluttered workspace—tabs open for deadlines, closed for dua. This is the paradox of the hustle: we trade the *eternal* for the ephemeral, mistaking burnout for ambition.

The Prophet's peace be upon him warning reverberates across centuries, a mirror held to our dissonance:

> *"Take benefit of five before five: Your youth before old age, your health before sickness, your wealth before poverty, your free time before preoccupation, and your life before death."*

Yet we auction these treasures to the highest bidder. Youth

is mortgaged to build résumés, health traded for stock options, wealth squandered on status symbols that rust before the next iPhone launch. Free time? A myth, outsourced to productivity apps that gamify rest. Even precious, singular life is fragmented into Zoom calls and inbox zero quests. We are the generation that *"optimises"* sleep but cannot name the last time we tasted the sweetness of Qiyam.

The Arithmetic of the Hollow

Hustle culture is a Ponzi scheme of the soul. We chase "passion projects" that drain our *Nafs* and "networking" that starves our humanity. The CEO prays Jumu'ah between mergers, and the entrepreneur fasts Ramadan between funding rounds—rituals reduced to pit stops in the race to nowhere. Allah asks for our hearts; we offer Him productivity journals.

And what do we reap? A generation drowning in existential static. We amass followers but lose connection, curate "authentic" personal brands while our true selves atrophy. The student who skipped Fajr graduate's First in her class, only to stare at her diploma, asking, *"Is this all?"* The Prophet's peace be upon him five gifts—youth, health, wealth, time, life—lie spent, like coins fed into a slot machine that never pays out.

Reclaiming the Currency of Worship

A Detour to Jannah

To worship is not to retreat from the world, but to recenter it. Imagine a life where deadlines bow to salah, where hustle fuels ibadah instead of eclipsing it. What if "success" meant standing before Allah with a heart unshackled from the anxiety of more?

The call is urgent: Delete the apps that measure your worth in likes. Let your soul breathe between adhan and email. The student who guards her Fajr may lose an hour of study, but she gains the One who says, *"I am as My servant expects Me to be."*

Allah did not create you to be a cog in capitalism's assembly line. You are a living ayah, a walking Miraj of purpose. The choice is yours: Chase the hustle's hollow hymns or let your soul rise in Sujood—the only act that fills the ledger with light.

"Who Am I?" in a World of Labels

Allah's call cuts through the cacophony of curated identities:

> *"O mankind, fear your Lord, who created you from one soul…" (Surah An-Nisa 4:1).*

One soul. One origin. One Creator. Yet modernity demands we shatter ourselves into shards of hashtags and hyphenated labels: *Liberal Muslim. Conservative Muslim. Cultural Muslim. Spiritual-but-not religious.* We are

20

pressured to curate personas like social media feeds—algorithmically optimised for approval, diluted for digestibility. Our fitrah, that divine imprint whispering *"Laa ilaha illallah"* in the marrow of our bones, is drowned out by the noise of performative belonging.

The Masks We Wear

Consider the brother who tucks his prayer mat into the closet of his corporate persona. At work, he silences his "Muslimness," scrubbing his speech of *Insha'Allah* and his calendar of Salah—terrified the scent of musk or the shadow of a beard might cost him a promotion. He laughs at jokes that curdle his conscience, nods at policies that clash with his creed, and slowly, the man in the mirror becomes a stranger. At home, he tells himself, *"I'll pray later."* But "later" gathers dust. Over time, Salah slips from obligation to inconvenience, then from inconvenience to relic—a childhood habit, like doodling in Quran margins. His faith, once a flowing river, evaporates into puddles of nostalgia.

The Prophet peace be upon him said,

> *"The believer is a mirror to the believer" (Abu Dawud).*

But how can we reflect one another when our surfaces are polished facades? We've turned *tawhid*—the oneness of Allah—into a fractured identity crisis.

The *Ummah*, meant to be a single body, now resembles a dismembered mannequin—a limb labelled "progressive," another "traditional," each part disowning the others.

The Algorithm of the Soul

Allah asks us to *know ourselves*, but the world trains us to *brand ourselves*. Fitrah is not a static label but a compass—a magnetic pull toward truth. Yet we let think pieces and Twitter threads reprogram our north. The "spiritual but not religious" Muslim chases transcendence through yoga retreats and astrology apps, mistaking borrowed mysticism for the Real. The "cultural Muslim" preserves Eid feasts but discards fasting, reducing Deen to a heritage museum. Each label is a cage, a reduction of the vastness Allah knit into your soul.

> *"And do not mix truth with falsehood or conceal the truth while you know" (Surah Al-Baqarah 2:42).*

But we mix truths daily. We splice Quranic verses into TED Talk aesthetics, strip the Seerah of its sacrifices to fit corporate leadership seminars, and silence the parts of our faith that "don't test well" in secular spaces. The brother who hides his prayers is not just compromising ritual—he's erasing his *self*. For when you amputate pieces of your soul to please others, you haemorrhage the essence Allah designed you to embody.

The Return to Fitrah

Allah's reminder— "created you from one soul"—is indictment and invitation. Indictment: *Why do you splinter what I unified?* Invitation: *Come home to your essence.* Fitrah is not a hashtag but a homing beacon. It's the student who prays Dhuhr in the office stairwell, not for performative piety, but because humility to Allah steels her spine in boardrooms. It's the father who cancels a networking event to weep with his son over Surah Ar-Rahman.

The Prophet's peace be upon him warning echoes:

> *"A time will come when holding onto your faith will be like clutching burning coals" (Tirmidhi).*

That time is now. To reclaim yourself, you must unlabel. Peel off the stickers of worldly approval. Let your soul breathe beyond binaries.

When you stand before Allah, He will not ask, *"What tribe did you belong to?"* but *"Did you belong to Me?"* The labels will melt like wax; only your scorched or shining heart will remain.

"The Myth of 'Having It All'

Shaytan's whisper slithers through our ambition like a snake in a boardroom: "You can balance Dunya and akhirah perfectly." It's a seductive lie, polished for the LinkedIn generation—a promise that you can "optimise" worship like a productivity hack, that Allah's pleasure fits neatly between PowerPoint slides and Pilates classes. But the Prophet peace be upon him dismantles this delusion with divine clarity:

> *"The dunya is cursed, and what is in it is cursed—except the remembrance of Allah and what He loves..."(Tirmidhi Hadith 2322)*

Yet we chase "balance" like a mirage in a desert of deadlines. We sprint through life's checklist: Fajr squeezed between snooze buttons, Athan apps muted during Zoom calls, halaqas attended with one eye on the clock. We volunteer to pad résumés, network to climb ladders, and cling to haram relationships, mistaking loneliness for love. All while curating a #Blessed facade—sunset selfies at the masjid, captioned with Ayah we no longer feel in our bones. The result? Not balance, but spiritual bankruptcy.

The Math of Exhaustion

Imagine the sister who prays five times a day—but her heart ticks like a metronome, counting minutes until she can return to emails. She reads Quran, but the words blur into background noise as her mind replays office politics. She attends halaqas, yet her takeaways are Instagram stories, not internalised wisdom. By night, she scrolls through Haram reels, numbing her guilt with dopamine hits. *"I'm doing it all!"* she insists, until her body rebels—

migraines, insomnia, a heart that forgets how to whisper *"Ya Rabb."* Burnout isn't a sign of weakness; it's the soul's protest against the tyranny of "having it all."

Shaytan's "balance" is a lie. He convinces us to invest everything in Dunya's fleeting returns, promising we'll cash out in akhirah later. But when the market of life crashes—and it always does—we're left with a portfolio of hollow rituals and stockpiled regrets. The Prophet peace be upon him's words ring truer now than ever:

> *"The Dunya is a prison for the believer and a paradise for the disbeliever" (Muslim).*

Yet we've redecorated our cells with Wi-Fi and called it freedom.

The #Blessed Deception

Social media sells salvation in filters and hashtags. We post Quran pages artfully strewn with coffee mugs, turning revelation into aesthetic. We hashtag #JummahMubarak while ignoring the Khutbah (sermon). The more we perform piety, the less we embody it. Shaytan doesn't need us to abandon Salah—just to rush it. He doesn't demand we reject Quran—just to recite it without letting it pierce our pride. He's content to watch us "have it all" while owning nothing of substance.

> *Allah warns: "Do not let your wealth and children distract you from the remembrance of Allah. For whoever does so—it is they who*

are the losers" (Surah Al-Munafiqun 63:9).

But we've inverted the equation: We use Allah to justify our distractions. *"Allah wants me to succeed!"* becomes license to skip Maghrib for meetings. *"He's the Most Merciful!"* morphs into complacency in sin. Yet the Prophet peace be upon him—who carried the weight of prophethood—still stood in prayer until his feet swelled, not because he lacked balance, but because he knew true success is measured in prostration, not promotions.

The Way Back: From Scarcity to Sufficiency

The remedy isn't monastic retreat but ruthless prioritisation. The Dunya is not cursed for existing but for being *prioritised*. What Allah loves—prayer with presence, charity with empathy, dhikr that stills the chaos—are the exceptions that redeem the world's curse.

To "have it all" is Shaytan's trap. To have *enough* is Allah's mercy. Let the missed promotion be the price of guarding Fajr. Let the quieter social life be the cost of a clean heart. The sister who cancels a networking event to weep in Tahajjud isn't falling behind—she's rebalancing her scales for the only Audit that matters.

> *Allah says: "Whoever turns away from My remembrance will have a life of narrowness…" (20:124).*

The choice is clear: Chase the mirage of "balance" and suffocate or surrender to the sufficiency of His remembrance—and breathe.

The Quiet Whispers of the Soul

Spiritual distance does not announce itself with fireworks. It begins as a faint unease—a quiet voice in your soul that whispers, *"Something isn't right."* Over time, if ignored, that whisper becomes a scream.

Here's how to listen and what to look out for before it's too late:

Numbness in Worship: Prayers Without Presence: You mechanically perform Salah—mouthing words your heart no longer feels. Duas become wish lists recited on autopilot. The Quran feels heavy in your hands, its verses blurring into ink on a page.

Example: *A brother rushes through Maghrib prayer, distracted by a Twitter feud. Later, he can't recall if he prayed three or four rak'ahs. The guilt makes him avoid praying altogether.*

Numbness is a warning: your soul is starving.
Chasing the Unquenchable: You hop from goal to goal— new degree, relationship, new hobby—but fulfilment stays out of reach. The more you achieve, the more restless you become.

Example: *A young man checks off society's milestones: graduate, marry, buy a house. Yet he lies awake at night, haunted by a question: "Why do I feel like I'm running in circles?"*

Have you ever reflected on Qarun (Korah), whose wealth and status made him boast, **"I was only given it because of the knowledge I have!"** (Surah Al-Qasas 28:78)? His treasures buried him alive—a metaphor for worldly pursuits that suffocate the soul.

The Voice You Keep Muting: A voice nags you when you gossip, skip prayer, or indulge in haram: *"This isn't you."* You silence it with excuses: *"I'll fix it later," "Everyone does it,"* or *"Allah will forgive me."*

Example: *A woman swears off a toxic relationship but drifts back whenever she feels lonely. She justifies it:"At least I'm not married to him." But the guilt follows her like a shadow.*

Allah's Warning:

> *"And do not be like those who forgot Allah,*
> *so He made them forget   themselves. It*
> *is they   who are defiantly disobedient"*
> *(Surah Al-Hashr 59:19).*

Guilt is a mercy—a compass pointing you home. Ignore it long enough, and you'll forget how to read it.

A Detour to Jannah

The Quran Collects Dust: Your Mushaf sits untouched on the shelf, its pages yellowing. You tell yourself, *"I'll read it when I have time,"* but "time" never comes. When you open it, the words feel distant, as if they're meant for someone else.

Example: *Ahmed used to begin every morning with the Quran, reciting a few pages before starting his day. But ever since life got busier—work, family, endless to-do lists—his Mushaf has been untouched on the shelf. The dust has gathered on the cover, and when he finally picks it up, the pages feel foreign in his hands. He flips through them, trying to reconnect, but the words seem distant. "Maybe tomorrow," he tells himself, closing it again. But deep down, he knows tomorrow keeps slipping further away.*

The Quran isn't just a book—it's a lifeline. Letting it gather dust is like refusing water in a desert.

Anger at Gentle Reminders: A friend suggests you join a halaqa, and you snap, *"Stop judging me!"* A parent asks if you've prayed, and you roll your eyes. Your anger isn't about them—it's about the truth you're avoiding.

Example: *Maya's mum asks, "Did you read the Quran today?" Maya rolls her eyes, snapping back, "I'm not a little kid, stop treating me like one." Her frustration is palpable, but it's not really about her mum. Later, her* *friend asks, "Have you prayed today?" Maya's temper flares again, "Why do you always ask me that?" The anger isn't about her mum or her friend but the truth she's been avoiding. She feels overwhelmed by everything, and the last thing she wants to face is the emptiness inside when it comes to her faith."*

Defensiveness is pride masking fear—fear that the reminders are right.

The Mercy in The Whisper: These signs are not condemnations but invitations. That aches in your chest, the guilt you can't shake, the Quran gathering dust. They're proof Allah hasn't given up on you. Your soul is begging you to return.

The Prophet peace be upon him said:

> *"Allah is more merciful to His servants than a mother is to her child" (Bukhari Hadith 5999).*

Even now, as you read these words, His mercy pulls you back. Will you let it?

The Anatomy of a Detour

A spiritual detour is rarely a single, dramatic wrong turn. It is a slow unravelling—a series of choices, compromises, and overlooked whispers of the soul that pull us away from the straight path. To understand why we drift, we must dissect the anatomy of a detour, layer by layer, through the lens of Islamic wisdom and human vulnerability.

Allah says:

> *"And do not approach immoralities—what is apparent of them and what is concealed"*
> *(Surah Al A'raf 6:151).*

Detours begin with seemingly harmless choices:

- **"Just this once"**: Skipping Fajr to catch up on sleep. Lying to avoid conflict. Watching a show with inappropriate scenes.
- **The Gradual Erosion:** Each compromise dulls the conscience. What once felt forbidden becomes normalised.

The Prophet peace be upon him warned:

> *"Beware of small sins! For they gather upon a person until they destroy him"* (Sunan Ibn Majah, Hadith 4245).

Like termites gnawing at a foundation, minor sins weaken our spiritual resolve until the structure collapses.

The Illusion of Control: "I'll Fix It Later": Shaytan's oldest trick is convincing us we have unlimited time. He whispers: *"Enjoy life now—repent when you're older, when you're*

31

A Detour to Jannah

married, when you're 'ready.'"

We trade eternal rewards for temporary pleasures, gambling with a future we're not guaranteed.

Allah says:

> "........My Lord if only You would delay me
> for a brief term so I would give charity and
> be among the righteous!'" (Surah Al-
> Munafiqun 63:10).

Tomorrow is a mirage. The only moment we own is *now.*

When the World Becomes a Drug: Allah says:

> "The life of this world is but
> amusement and diversion…" (Surah Al-
> Hadid 6:32).

The Dunya addicts us through:

- **Comparison Trap:** Social media fuels envy— *"Why can't I have their lifestyle, their freedom?"*
- **Materialism:** We chase status symbols (cars, clothes, careers) to fill a void only Allah can fill.

Example: A brother works 80-hour weeks, climbing the corporate ladder. He achieves his goals but loses his marriage, health, and connection to Allah.

The Prophet peace be upon him said:

> "Richness is not in having many possessions.
> True richness is the richness of the soul"
> (Sahih Muslim, Hadith 1051).

Yet we starve our souls to feast our eyes.

Allah says:

> *"Are those who know equal to those who do not know?" (Surah Az-Zumar 39:9).*

Spiritual decay thrives in the absence of knowledge:

- **Neglecting Quran and Sunnah:** Our faith becomes brittle without daily nourishment from the Quran or prophetic teachings.
- **Misplaced Priorities:** We memorise TikTok trends but forget Surah Al-Fatihah.

In most cases ignorance isn't bliss—it's a slow death of the heart.

Shaytan's Playbook: Exploiting Human Weakness:

Shaytan doesn't need grand gestures to lead us astray. He weaponises:

- **Doubt:** *"Does Allah care if I pray?"*

- **Despair:** *"I've messed up too much—He'll never forgive me."*
- **Distraction:** Keeping us too busy to reflect, too tired to pray.

Allah warns:

> *"Indeed, Satan is an enemy to you, so take*
> *him as an enemy. He only invites his*
> *party to be companions of the Blaze"*
> *(Surah Fatir 35:6).*

Yet we treat him like a harmless prankster, not the sworn enemy he is.

When We Stop Asking for Help:

The Prophet peace be upon him said:

> *"Dua is the essence of worship" (At-Tirmidhi, Hadith 3371).*

Detours solidify when we rely on ourselves instead of Allah:

- **Pride:** *"I can handle this alone."*
- **Resignation:** *"It's too late to change."*

Stories of Straying and Returning

Detours often mark the journey of faith, but the Quran and Sunnah are replete with stories of those who strayed and found their way back through Allah's infinite mercy. These narratives offer hope and guidance, reminding us that redemption is always within reach.

A Tale of Wealth and Humility (Surah Al-Kahf 18:32-42)

A wealthy man, blessed with two lush gardens, boasted to his companion, "**I am greater than you in wealth and might!**" (Quran 18:34). Consumed by pride, he dismissed the transient nature of worldly blessings and forgot to attribute his success to Allah. Overnight, his gardens were destroyed—a divine reminder that proper sustenance comes only from Allah. Humbled, he cried, "**If only I had not associated anyone with my Lord!**" **(Quran 18:42).**

Lesson:

Material wealth and status can blind us to our reliance on Allah, but humility and repentance restore our sight.

Reflection:

- What worldly blessings do I take for granted? How can I practice gratitude daily?

Musa (AS) in Midian: From Exile to Purpose (Surah Al-Qasas 28:15-28)

After fleeing Egypt, Musa (AS) arrived in Midian— exhausted, alone, and uncertain of his future. He helped two women water their flock, an act of kindness that led to marriage, stability, and time for reflection. Years later, Allah called him to the burning bush, transforming his exile into a mission: *"Go to Pharaoh, for he has transgressed"* (Quran 20:24).

Lesson:

Even in moments of displacement, Allah prepares us for a

greater purpose. Detours can be divine appointments.

Reflection:

- Have I ever felt lost, only to discover a new path through faith?

- How can I trust Allah's plan during uncertainty?

A Modern Return

Adam, a college student, abandoned Salah and indulged in parties to "fit in." Over time, guilt gnawed at him. One night, he stumbled upon a Quran app and randomly opened Surah Ar-Rahman: *"So which of the favours of your Lord would you deny?"* (Surah Ar-Rahman 55:13). Overwhelmed, he wept and phoned his father: "Can you teach me to pray again?"

Lesson:
No matter how far we wander, Allah's signs—a verse, a memory, a parent's love—can reignite our faith.

Reflection:

- What "signs" has Allah placed in my life to guide me back?

- Who can I turn to for support in rebuilding my faith?

The Woman Who Reclaimed Her Hijab

Aisha removed her hijab after facing workplace discrimination. But years later, her daughter asked, "Why don't you cover your hair like Grandma?"

The question pierced her heart. After a lot of dua and soul searching, she slowly reintroduced the hijab, finding strength in online communities of Muslim women.

Lesson:

Societal pressures may lead us astray, but sincere intention and community support anchor us.

Reflection:

- How do external pressures influence my choices?

- How can I foster a supportive faith community?

The Gift of Awareness

Acknowledging you're lost is the first step toward being found. The fact that this chapter stirs something in you— regret, recognition, or even resistance— is a sign that your heart is still alive with Iman.

The Prophet peace be upon him said:

> *"Verily, when the believer commits a sin, a black spot covers his heart. If he repents, stops the sin, and seeks forgiveness, his heart is polished.* But if he increases in sin, the spot increases…"* (Ibn Majah Hadith 4244).

That "polish" isn't out of reach. The straight path may feel distant, but it's still there, waiting for you to take the first step back.

Reflective Exercises

These exercises are designed to meet you where you are—whether in guilt, numbness, or hope—and guide you toward honest self-reflection and actionable change. You can choose to do them all or just one.

The Mirror of Regret and Hope

Purpose: Confront the cost of your detour while rekindling hope in Allah's mercy.

Steps:

1. Stand before a physical mirror.
2. Speak aloud: *"This is the face of someone who has made mistakes. But this is also the face of someone Allah still loves."*
3. Write down one regret (e.g., abandoning prayer, compromising values).
4. Beside it, write **one Quranic verse** that offers hope (e.g., Surah Az-Zumar 39:53).

Reflection: *"How can I let Allah's mercy outweigh my regret today?"*

The Forgiveness Dialogue

Purpose: Release self-condemnation and embrace Allah's forgiveness.

Steps:

1. Write a letter to Allah detailing a sin or regret. Be brutally honest.
2. Write Allah's response using Quranic verses (e.g., *"O My servants who have transgressed against themselves, do not despair..."*).
3. Burn or bury the letter as a symbol of release

"Ya Allah, I've wandered far. Guide my feet, soften my heart, and light my way back to You. Let my detour become a testimony of Your mercy. Amee

CHAPTER TWO
THE PURPOSE OF BEING LOST

Imagine a seed buried in darkness. To the untrained eye, it appears lost—trapped beneath layers of soil, cut off from the sun. Yet, in that stillness, it is being transformed. Roots stretch downwards, anchoring it. A stem pushes upwards, guided by an invisible compass. What seems like confinement is, in truth, the very process that enables it to rise stronger and taller than ever before.

You're in this sacred tension as well. The ache of disconnection you experience—the distance from the path you once knew—doesn't signify abandonment. It represents transformation.

In Chapter 1, you began to trace the contours of your detour: the choices that led you here, the quiet unease of drifting, the mirror that reflected a stranger's face. Now, we turn to the question that lingers like dawn on the horizon: *Why?*

Why would a Merciful Lord allow His servants to lose their way?

The answer lies not in the destination but in the journey itself. In His infinite wisdom, Allah designs detours not to punish but to polish. To break the illusion of self-sufficiency. To turn wanderers into warriors of faith.

Consider the story of Hajar (RA), who is left in the barren desert of Mecca with her infant son Ismail. With only her trust in Allah, she ran between Safa and Marwa, desperate for water. Her literal *lostness* became the birthplace of Zamzam—a wellspring of mercy that flows to this day. Her struggle is a pillar of our Hajj.

This chapter is an invitation to reframe your wilderness. Through Quranic parables, prophetic wisdom, and the raw honesty of modern souls who've wandered, you'll discover:

- How trials carve space in the heart for deeper faith.
- Why the most profound growth often begins in the soil of struggle.
- How to spot Allah's hidden compass— even in the darkest detours.

The Prophet peace be upon him said:

> *"How wonderful is the affair of the believer!*
> *His matter is always good....If something*
> *good happens to him, he is grateful, and that*
> *is good for him. If something bad happens to*
> *him, he is patient, and that is good for him*
> *(Muslim Hadith 2999.)*

Your "lostness" is not a flaw—it's a testament to your humanity and Allah's divine plan. Let's unravel its purpose together.

My dear reader, let me share some Quranic stories that touched my heart and I hope you might connect with. Perhaps you see yourself in them, or maybe they'll provide you with a sense of belonging.

Adam (AS): The First Detour and the Birth of Mercy

Adam (AS) and Hawwa (RA) tasted the forbidden tree, disobeying Allah in Jannah. Expelled to Earth, they were engulfed in guilt and regret. Their detour was not just a fall—it was the first human experience of separation from Allah.

The Purpose:
Allah taught them the language of repentance so that we can use it today:

> *"Our Lord, we have wronged ourselves, and if You do not forgive us and have mercy upon us, we will surely be among the losers"*
> *(Surah Al-A'raf 7:23).*

Their story became a blueprint for humanity: *No sin is beyond Allah's forgiveness if followed by sincere Tawbah.*

Reflection:
What "forbidden tree" have you chased, and how can

Adam's repentance inspire your return?

I understand you might think this is about a prophet and the people chosen by Allah. What about some modern-day parables that we can all benefit from reflecting on?

Layla's Empty Cradle: When Grief Creates a Bridge to Allah

Layla's arms ached with the weight of emptiness. After three miscarriages, her womb felt like a grave, and her prayers dissolved into silence. She stopped attending the Mosque, unable to bear the sight of mothers cradling their babies. "Why would Allah let me love something He'd just take?" she'd whisper, staring at the nursery she'd painted sky-blue.

The Divine Design:

One winter night, she stumbled upon an old journal. A faded entry read: *"Today, I held my niece and thanked Allah for the joy of loving, even briefly."* Beneath it, a Quranic verse she'd once clung to:

> *"And We will surely test you with something of fear and hunger and loss... But give good tidings to the patient" (Surah Al- Baqarah 2:155).*

Tears blurred the ink as she realised that her grief wasn't proof of Allah's absence—it was proof of His trust in her to love *fearlessly*, even when it hurt. Today, Layla is a kindergarten teacher, nurturing, loving, caring for future generations and reflecting Allah's Mercy on others.

Reflection:

What heartbreak have you buried instead of offering to Allah?

Aisha's Mask: The Instagram Life That Almost Stole Her Soul

Aisha's hijab became a prop. She'd pose in pastel abayas for 50k followers, then peel them off like costumes for parties where no one knew her name. "Muslim influencer" felt like a lie—until the night a DM pierced her facade: *"Sister, I started praying because of you. Are you okay?"*

The Divine Design:

She deleted her account. For the first time in years, she prayed without filming it. Now, she teaches girls to seek Allah's applause, not the world's.

Reflection:

What masks are you wearing? Who would you be if the world stopped watching?

Yusuf's Prison: Wrongfully Accused, Unexpectedly Freed

The Detour:
Yusuf spent five years in a cell the size of a prayer mat, convicted of a crime he didn't commit. Anger rotted his faith. *"Where's Your justice?"* he'd scream at the walls. Then, one day, his wife brought him a crumpled Quran. He read Surah Yusuf and sobbed—his namesake

prophet was betrayed, imprisoned, and *still* trusted Allah's plan.

The Divine Design:

Freed by new evidence, Yusuf now fights for the innocent. "Prison taught me freedom isn't out there," he says, tapping his chest. "It's here—in surrender to Allah."

Reflection:

What "prison" have you built with your own hands? Could it be your path to emancipation?

How Patience Transforms Pain

The Prophet's peace be upon him promise is radical in an age that pathologises pain:

"No fatigue, illness, anxiety, sorrow, harm, or sadness befalls a Muslim—even a thorn that pricks them—without Allah expiating their sins because of it." (Bukhari, 5641).

Yet we live in a world scrambling to anaesthetise struggle. Therapy apps promise to "fix" grief in six sessions, TikTok gurus sell "toxic positivity" as cure-alls, and pharmacies peddle pills to mute every discomfort. But what if our pains are not glitches to erase, but portals to purification? Sabr is not passive endurance—it is active alchemy, transmuting leaden trials into golden scars that glint with divine purpose.

The Furnace of Humility

Arrogance suffocates in the furnace of suffering. When chronic illness saps your strength, you can't muscle through with self-reliance. When layoffs shatter your career identity, you can't hustle to invincibility. Sabr begins here—in the rubble of our delusions of control. The mother rocking her autistic child through midnight meltdowns, the brother bankrupted by betrayal, the student failing despite grinding day and night—all kneel in the same classroom: *"La hawla wa la quwwata illa billah."* No power except by Allah. Trials don't just teach humility; they *enforce* it, sanding down the ego's jagged edges until we fit into the mould of surrender.

Trust as Rebellion

Tawakkul is not spiritual complacency but radical defiance. In a culture that worships hustle as holiness, choosing to say *"Allah is sufficient for me"* is an act of rebellion. Consider the father diagnosed with cancer who prays, *"You are the Healer, but I accept whatever You decree,"* then donates his treatment fund to orphans. Or the refugee who loses everything but whispers *"Alhamdulillah"* upon seeing the sunrise. Tawakkul is not blind fatalism—it is *seeing* Allah's Hand in the storm and grabbing hold. Each trial is a sparring match to strengthen our reliance muscles; every unanswered dua a test to deepen our *Yaqeen* that Allah's "not right now" is a divine redirection.

Gratitude in the Wound

Pain rewires our vision. The migraineur learns to praise

the days without throbbing. The divorcee treasures solitude's quiet over a toxic marriage's noise. The infertile couple finds joy in pouring love into nieces and strangers. Sabr excavates buried blessings: the miracle of a functioning kidney, the luxury of safety, the gift of a mind unhaunted by trauma. As the poet wrote: *"You never know what is enough until you know what is more than enough."*

Fatima's Unlearning

When Fatima lost her corporate job, she raged at Allah—*"I tithed, I prayed Tahajjud, I followed the rules!"* For weeks, she scrolls LinkedIn obsessively, her self-worth tied to rejection emails. Then one Fajr, sleep-deprived and desperate, she opens the Quran randomly to Surah Taha: *"And I chose you for Myself"* (20:41).

Slowly, she unlearns. Unemployment becomes her *khalwa* (retreat). She memorises Surah Ad-Duha with her children, their voices stitching her fractured heart. She cooks meals for a single mother neighbour, discovering the *barakah* of time she'd once sold to corporations. *"I thought I lost my income,"* she laughs now, *"but Allah fired me from a prison I didn't know I'd built."* Her résumé gap? A bridge to her true self.

The Door That Never Rusts: Tawbah as Oxygen

Allah's invitation defies human logic:

> *"Say, 'O My servants who have transgressed against themselves, do not despair of the mercy of Allah..."(Surah Az-Zumar 39:53)*

We, who cancel people for decade-old tweets, can't fathom a mercy that embraces even deathbed repentance. The hadith tells of the man who murdered 99 souls yet was forgiven when he took one step toward Allah. It speaks of the idolater who, in his final breath, cried *"You are the Lord of the heavens!"* and entered Paradise. Our human courts demand life sentences: Allah's Court offers life *re*-sentences.

The Anatomy of Divine Amnesty

- **No Sin Too Great**: The porn addict who sobs into his prayer mat, the sister who aborted in panic, the liar whose tongue destroyed families—all find the same door open. Allah does not tally crimes; He weighs sincerity.
- **No Delay Too Late**: The gangster who memorises Quran on death row, the CEO who quits haram earnings to die penniless but clean, the addict who prays his first Salah in rehab—all are proof: Tawbah is not a reward for the worthy, but oxygen for the drowning.

The Calculus of Scars

Sabr transforms pain not by removing it, but by redeeming it. Every chronic illness becomes a lifelong Zakat of patience. Every betrayal, a workshop in forgiveness. Every loss, a space for Allah to pour what He's withheld. The Prophet peace be upon him didn't say trials *avoid* us—he said they *cleanse* us.

So let the world pop pills and curse the thorns. The believer tends their wounds with *Alhamdulillah*, knowing each scar is a receipt of sins erased, a roadmap to the Only One who turns our *"Why me?"* into *"Use me."*

The Whisper of Hope:

Allah says: *"And whoever fears Allah—He will make for him a way out and provide for him from where he does not expect." (Surah At- Talaq 65:2-3)*

No trial is endless, and no detour is permanent. When facing difficulties, remember that Allah always provides a way out. Help and guidance may come from the most unexpected places—through a stranger's kindness, a sudden insight, a book (like this one), or even a verse from the Qur'an that speaks directly to your heart. Trust that relief will come when you least expect it and always keep faith that Allah's mercy and provision are limitless.

Turning Detours into Worship:

The Daily "Sacred Pause"

What to Do:

Carve out 5 minutes each morning to sit in silence. Close your eyes, place a hand over your heart, and ask: *"What is Allah teaching me in this season of my life?"*

Why It Works:

Intentional stillness creates space for divine insight. Unlike rushed prayers, this practice trains you to *listen* for answers rather than demand them.

This is a practice that you might still be doing in 20 years. It never gets old. I find myself doing it many times during my day when I am confused, angered, or in doubt. I know Allah is teaching me something; I just have to listen.

The "Habit Stacking" Strategy

What to Do:

Pair small acts of worship with daily routines:

Recite *"SubhanAllah"* 10 times while brushing your teeth.

- Whisper a dua for guidance while waiting for your coffee to brew.
- Practice gratitude during your commute: *"Alhamdulillah for this car, this road, this breath."*

Why It Works:

Anchoring worship to habits makes spirituality sustainable, even in chaos

---

The "Gratitude Mapping" Exercise

What to Do:

1. Draw a circle in the center of a page labelled "This Detour."
2. Branching out, write:

   - Lessons Learned (e.g., humility, resilience).
   - Unexpected Blessings (e.g., new friendships, clarity).
   - Skills Gained (e.g., self-forgiveness).

Why It Works: Visualising growth reframes your detour as

a curriculum designed by Allah.

The "Legacy Thinking" Mindset

What to Do:

Ask yourself daily: *"If I died today, what would this detour teach others about Allah's mercy?"*

Why It Works:

Shifting focus from *"Why me?"* to *"How can this serve?"* transforms pain into purpose

---

The "Micro-Ibadah" Experiment

What to Do:

Commit to one tiny, consistent act of worship for 40 days:

- Recite "Astaghfirullah" 100 times before bed.
- Donate $1 daily to a cause.
- Send one encouraging text to a struggling friend.

Why It Works:

Small, sustainable actions rebuild spiritual momentum without overwhelming you.

The Dawn After the Darkness

Your detour is not the end—it's a bridge. Imagine a river

forced to bend around mountains: its twists are not mistakes, but the path that carves valleys into existence. So too, your struggles—those winding, uncertain roads—are not signs of failure. They are *sacred architecture*, designed by Allah to lead you not *away* from Him, but *toward* Him. Every step through this wilderness, every stumble in the dark, draws you closer to His mercy, even when your heart screams, *"I am alone."* That scream is a prayer—a raw, unpolished *dua* He collects like pearls. You are not lost. You are *found*—not in the safety of familiar shores but in the classroom of divine love. Here, the curriculum is written in tears and trials, the lessons etched with questions that ache. Yet this is where hearts are remade: in the friction between doubt and faith, between *"Why me?"* and *"Use me."*

The Prophet peace be upon him taught that when Allah loves a servant, He tests them—not to break them, but to *break open* the parts they've sealed off: pride, self-reliance, and the illusion of control. What feels like exile is enrolment in a school where the ultimate degree is *nearness to Him.*

> *"Ya Allah, turn my wounds into wisdom, my trials into triumph, and my detours into direct paths to You. Let my struggle be the ink that writes my story of return. Ameen."*

CHAPTER THREE
A MAP FOR REFLECTION

Feeling spiritually adrift can bring about a unique and profound loneliness beyond the simple absence of direction. It is the silence where vibrant, comforting faith once hummed; the hollow ache of prayers faltering in the air, unheard and unfulfilled; and the quiet, pervasive shame of asking oneself, "How did I get here?" This feeling of isolation, of being untethered, is an experience I know all too well.

Many moons ago, I was in a dimly lit room that never felt like mine. The space was barren and uninviting, with a prayer rug tucked away in a corner, gathering layers of dust that seemed to mirror the neglect I had begun to show my spiritual self. I had started praying sporadically months earlier—for reasons I can't pinpoint. Life had become a blur of relentless deadlines, packed trains, and conversations that left me increasingly empty. I began to lose sight of who I was in the midst of a daily grind that felt devoid of meaning.

One night, after hours of mindlessly scrolling through my phone until dawn, the overwhelming emptiness finally crashed on me. In the solitude of that long, sleepless night, I found myself whispering into the darkness, *"Is this it? Is this who I've become?"* Heavy with despair, the question hung as I realised I was lost. I was lost not because I didn't know the way back to a more fulfilling life but because I no longer recognised the person I had once been—the person who used to cry during dua, who found solace in the rhythmic recitation of Surah Ar-Rahman, and who believed with unshakable certainty that Allah was nearby.

In that season of wandering, as I navigated through the fog of my own making, I learned an invaluable lesson: feeling lost is not a sign of weakness but a deeply human experience. Even the Prophets, whom we revere and look up to, faced moments of doubt, stumbled in their journeys and wept in the darkness of their trials. Their stories remind us that our detours do not define us; what truly matters is our willingness to pause, reflect, and allow Allah's light to guide us back to the path of righteousness.

This chapter is for the part of you tired of pretending, for those moments when faith feels like a forgotten language—a language you once spoke fluently but now struggle to recall. It is for those nights when you lie awake, wondering if Allah still hears your desperate calls and if He still cares about the silent cries of your heart. Together, let us embark on a journey to chart your return, not to judge the distance you have wandered, but to illuminate the unique path that only you can tread back to the home of your soul.

A Detour to Jannah

Know that every moment of doubt and every tear shed in the darkness is a stepping stone towards rediscovery. Embrace your vulnerability as a sign of your humanity, and let it be the catalyst that rekindles the spark of faith within you. Even in the midst of despair, remember that Allah's mercy is infinite, and His guidance is always within reach. Your journey back is not a retreat—it is a courageous stride towards a renewed connection with the Divine, where every faltering step brings you closer to the peace only faith can offer.

The Prophet peace be upon him said:

> *Take account of yourselves before you are taken to account." (Tirmidhi Hadith 2540)*

How to Use This Chapter

The exercises here are not about tallying sins or wallowing in regret. They're about **clarity, compassion, and courage**. You'll:

1. **Assess where you are** with honesty, not shame.
2. **Trace the turning points** that led you here.
3. **Rediscover the thread of hope** Allah has woven into your story.

Think of this as your spiritual GPS—sometimes, you must acknowledge you are lost before rerouting.

> *A Dua for the Journey:*
>
> *Ya Allah, I'm standing in the wreckage of my*

own choices, and I don't know how to fix this.
But I'm here. I'm trying. Meet me in this
mess, and guide me back to You—one breath,
step, and prayer at a time. Ameen.

Where Are You Now?

The Faith Temperature Check

1. Rate your spiritual state on a scale of 1–10 (1 = disconnected, 10 = deeply connected).

2. Write down three reasons for your rating. Example:

- *"I pray regularly but feel distracted."*

- *"I've stopped reading the Quran but still feel drawn to Allah."*

3. Ask: *"What's one small step I can take to move closer to a 10?"*

Why It Works:

This exercise provides a snapshot of your spiritual health, helping you identify areas for growth without judgment

Mapping Your Spiritual Milestones

1. Draw a horizontal line across a page.
2. Label the left end *"Birth"* and the right end *"Now."*
3. Mark key moments that shaped your faith:

o **Highs:** Moments of closeness to Allah (e.g., memorising a surah, a powerful dua).

o **Lows:** Moments of distance (e.g., abandoning prayer, losing a loved one).

4. Reflect: *"What patterns do I see? How have my highs and lows shaped my relationship with Allah?"*

Why It Works:

Visualising your journey helps you see Allah's hand in every

twist and turn.

The 5 Pillars Check-In:

- **Shahadah:** Do I truly live by *"La ilaha illa Allah"?*
- **Salah:** Am I praying with presence and consistency?
- **Zakat:** Am I giving generously and purifying my wealth?
- **Sawm:** Do I fast beyond Ramadan, practising self-discipline?
- **Hajj:** Have I prepared

For each pillar, write: *"One thing I'm doing well"* and *"One area I can improve."*

Why It Works:

This structured reflection ensures a holistic assessment of your faith.

The Emotional and Spiritual Audit

1. List five emotions you've felt most often in the past month (e.g., anxiety, joy, guilt).

For each emotion, ask:

- *"What triggered this feeling?"*
- *"How did I respond?"*
- *"What does this reveal about my relationship with Allah?"*

2. End with a dua: *"Ya Allah, guide my heart to what pleases You."*

Why It Works:

Emotions are windows into the soul. This exercise helps you align your heart with Allah's will.

The Hidden Blessings List

1. Write down three challenges you're currently facing.
2. Beside each, list:

- *"What this struggle is teaching me."*
- *"One hidden blessing in this trial."*

Example:

- *Challenge:* "I lost my job."
- *Lesson:* "I'm learning to rely on Allah, not my salary."
- *Blessing:* "I have more time to spend with my family."

Why It Works:

Gratitude shifts your focus from what's missing to what's present, opening your heart to Allah's wisdom.

Reflection is not a one-time exercise—it's a lifelong practice. As you revisit these tools, remember:

Honesty is Healing: Acknowledge your struggles without shame.

Growth is Gradual: Small, consistent steps lead to lasting change.

Allah is Your Guide: He placed these questions in your heart to lead you home.

PART TWO: REORIENTING THE HEART.

CHAPTER FOUR
THE COMPASS OF TAWBAH

There comes a moment in every return journey when the soul whispers, "Enough." Enough running. Enough hiding. Enough of carrying the weight of regret like a stone in your chest. It's the time when the walls you've built around your heart begin to crack, and the light of Allah's mercy starts to seep through. Tawbah—repentance—is that sacred moment when you drop the stone, turn your face to Allah, and allow His mercy to lift you from the dirt of your mistakes.

I remember the first time I truly understood Tawbah. I was 21, sitting on the floor of a cramped bedroom, clutching prayer beads I hadn't touched in years. My life was a mess of broken promises—to Allah, to my family, to myself. I had strayed far from the path I once knew, and the distance felt impossible to bridge. That night, I whispered "Astaghfirullah" through tears, unsure if I deserved to say it. But Allah's reply wasn't a thunderous rebuke. It was a quiet, unshakable certainty: "You are forgiven."

That moment didn't fix everything. It didn't erase the years of neglect or the habits I'd formed. But it was the first step—the first time I believed that Allah's mercy was bigger than my mistakes. And that's what *Tawbah* is: not a magic eraser, but a compass. It doesn't promise you'll never get lost again but ensures you'll always find your way back.

This chapter is your invitation to rise.

Together, we will explore the following:

- What Tawbah truly means—beyond guilt, toward grace.
- Stories of those who stumbled but found their way back through Allah's mercy.
- Practical steps to make repentance a daily practice, not a one-time event.

So, you're seeking Tawbah—a fresh start, a chance to turn a new page in your life story. But what, exactly, is Tawbah?

Tawbah is far more than a fleeting act or a one time declaration. It is a continuous, heartfelt return to Allah, a soulful journey of repentance that calls for sincerity and humility at every step. As the Prophet peace be upon him reminded us:

> *"Every son of Adam sins, and the best of those who sin are those who repent."*

(Tirmidhi Hadith 4251)

These words invite you to understand that while sin is an inevitable part of our human journey, repentance is our greatest strength.

Tawbah is not:

- **A one-time event:** It isn't a checkbox you mark off after a moment of regret.
- **A transaction to erase guilt:** It doesn't work like a receipt you collect to cancel your wrongs.
- **A guarantee you'll never stumble again:** It is not a magical shield that promises no mistakes in the future.

Instead, Tawbah is:

- **A daily return to Allah:** Each day is a fresh opportunity to realign your heart with His light, regardless of yesterday's missteps.
- **A relationship restored:** It's about renewing your connection with the Divine, recognising that Allah's mercy is a constant embrace waiting for you.
- **A compass that reorients your heart toward His light:** Tawbah guides you back to a state of clarity and inner peace during life's turbulence.

You read that correctly—Tawbah is a daily practice, a constant return to Allah. Even the Prophet peace be upon him, in his perfect humility, sought forgiveness many times a day. This ongoing act of repentance isn't a reflection of weakness; it's a testament to a deep, living relationship with Allah.

Like every precious part of our faith, sincere repentance has its own structure, a spiritual anatomy. Allah invites us in the Qur'an:

> *"O you who believe, turn to Allah with sincere repentance…" (Surah At- Tahrim 66:8)*

This call to return is built upon what is called the *Three Pillars of Tawbah:*

1. **Acknowledgment:**

    The first step is to face your actions with honesty. Say it out loud or write it down: "I did this. I own it." Without excuses, you must name the sin and recognise its reality. This honest admission is the foundation upon which healing is built.

2. **Remorse:**

    Let your heart break, but do not despair. This is not about fear of punishment but deep, heartfelt sorrow for actions that tarnish the beauty of His creation. When you genuinely feel the weight of your missteps, that sorrow becomes the seed of transformation, softening the hardened parts of your soul.

3. **Commitment:**

   Finally, commit to taking tangible steps to avoid repeating the same mistakes. Tawbah calls for action—a promise to change that is as real as it is challenging. Whether seeking counsel, setting new boundaries, or engaging in acts that realign you with Allah's guidance, your commitment bridges remorse and redemption.

Two Journeys of Tawbah and the Mercy That Never Sleeps

Aisha's Exodus from Emptiness

Aisha's story is not one of rebellion, but erosion—a slow leaching of faith by the acid rain of cultural performativity. For years, she wore "Muslim" as a label, not a lifeline. Prayer became a childhood artifact, hijab a costume she shed for corporate boardrooms, and Ramadan a hashtag (#Blessed) devoid of meaning. The world fed her lies like candy: *"Empowerment is autonomy from Allah." "Success is a soul sold in pieces for promotions."* She swallowed them, mistaking the numbness of distraction for peace.

But the heart knows its Maker. In quiet moments—staring at neon city lights from her high-rise apartment, scrolling through filtered lives on Instagram—the void yawned. It whispered in the language of her fitrah: *"Is this all?"*

Her return began not with a bang, but a whimper. One Ramadan, driven by a hunger no takeout could satisfy, she wandered into a mosque—a stranger in her own skin. The scent of musk and old prayer carpets unravelled her. She crumpled in a corner, tears pooling on her blouse, her Gucci handbag clashing with the worn carpet. Shame metastasised: *"How dare I come here? After the nights I'd wasted, the haram I'd normalised, the prayers I'd mocked?"*

An elderly woman approached—face mapped with wrinkles like Quranic margins, hands trembling but heart steady. Without judgment, she pressed dates into Aisha's palm, a silent echo of the Prophet's peace be upon him's sunnah. Then, with a voice weathered by decades of dhikr, she breathed: *"Allah missed you more than you missed Him."*

Those words were a thunderclap. Aisha had expected scorn, sermons, or pity—not *mercy.* Not the revelation that Allah's longing for His creation outstrips their fleeting guilt. In that moment, the veils fell: Tawbah was not a courtroom where she'd be sentenced, but a homecoming. The doors weren't merely "open"— they'd *never been locked.*

The Aftermath: From Ashes to Anchor

Today, Aisha's LinkedIn reads *"Content Creator,"* but her true work unfolds in mosque basements and coffee shops. She leads halaqas for "Cultural Muslims" like her former self, dissecting Ayahs with the urgency of someone who's tasted hell's outskirts. *"I used to think 'sincerity' was for Islam influencers,"* she tells them. *"Now I know the difference between praying at Allah and praying to Him."*

Her hijab, once abandoned, now hangs like a banner of surrender—not to men's gazes, but to her Maker's grace. She laughs freely, unafraid of wrinkles, because her worth isn't pixel deep. The emptiness that once gnawed? Filled not by Allah's absolution, but His *affection*.

The Lesson: Mercy's Quantum Physics

Allah's calculus defies human math. We tally sins; He multiplies forgiveness. We measure distance; He spans galaxies to meet us. The Quran whispers this in Surah Az-Zumar: *"Do they not know that Allah accepts repentance from His servants?"* (9:104).

But Aisha's story teaches a subtler truth: **Tawbah is not a transaction—it's a transfusion**. It's not erasing your past, but letting Allah rewrite your future with the ink of His Rahma. The Prophet peace be upon him said, *"Allah is more joyous at the repentance of His servant than a man who loses his camel in a desert, then finds it"* (Bukhari). Imagine—the Creator of supernovas, giddy over *you* stumbling home.

The Weight of Shame: When the Prisoner Forgets the Key is in Their Hand

Shaytan's greatest trick isn't tempting us to sin—convincing us we're too filthy to bathe in mercy. We cradle shame like a crown of thorns, whispering: *"I've crossed a line… I've broken too much… I'm unlovable."* We tattoo "Haram" on our souls, forgetting Allah's promise: *"My mercy encompasses all things"* (7:156).

But here's the divine irony: **Guilt is the first sign your fitrah still breathes**. The dead feel no guilt. That ache? It's your soul's GPS screaming: *"Recalculating! Turn back to Mercy!"*

Aisha's tears in the mosque weren't weakness—they were liquid Tawbah, dissolving the rust on her heart. The Quran reframes guilt as sacred: *"Those who, when they commit an immorality or wrong themselves, remember Allah and seek forgiveness… and who forgives sins except Allah?"* (3:135).

The Anatomy of a Comeback

1. **Acknowledgment**: Not just *"I messed up,"* but *"I'm tired of being my own jailer."*
2. **Remorse**: Tears that water the seeds of change.
3. **Return**: The courage to limp toward Allah, as the prodigal son did.
4. **Reconstruction**: Letting mercy repurpose your pain into a compass for others.

The Invitation: Your Turn

Dear sister/brother—yes, *sister/brother*, for your courage in reading this far has knit us as kin—this is your sign. That secret sin you've caged in silence? The addiction you've numbed with Netflix? The prayer you've postponed for a promotion? Allah isn't waiting to judge you. He's waiting to *embrace* you.

Allah's door has no handle because it only opens from the inside. Turn the knob of your heart. Walk through.

The Illusion of Self-Sufficiency: "I'll Fix Myself First"

After the initial sting of shame subsides, another subtle enemy of Tawbah surfaces—the false sense of self-sufficiency. It whispers in the quietest corners of our hearts, *"I'll fix myself first. I need to clean up my act before I can approach Allah."* This voice convinces us that we have the strength, we lack the resources or even the time to mend our brokenness on our own. This creates an illusion of control, as if we could somehow return to Allah when we've got ourselves together. Yet, in that moment, we unknowingly build a wall between ourselves and the very source of healing we desperately need.

Allah's call, however, is far more compassionate and inclusive. He doesn't wait for us to perfect ourselves; He invites us to come as we are. His words in the Qur'an are not just a plea; they are a loving embrace that reaches deep into our souls:

> *"Say, 'O My servants who have transgressed*
> *against themselves [by sinning], do not*
> *despair of the mercy of Allah. Indeed, Allah*
> *forgives all sins. Indeed, it is He who is the*
> *Forgiving, the Merciful.'" (Surah Az-Zumar*
> *39:53)*

This divine invitation reminds us that Tawbah is not about fixing ourselves first but turning to Allah as we are—broken, imperfect, and in desperate need of His mercy. It's about letting go of our pride and acknowledging that we cannot heal ourselves alone. True transformation begins not in our ability to "get it together" but in our willingness to surrender our self-reliance and lean fully on Allah's boundless mercy and love.

By accepting this call, we open ourselves to the change only Allah can bring about in our hearts. Through His guidance and nurturing, we are restored; through His mercy, we are truly transformed. When we surrender to His will, we are reminded that our strength is not in our independence but in our dependence on Him. We find the strength to rise, grow, and heal in that dependence.

The Fear of Relapse: "What If I Fail Again?"

And then there's that nagging fear: *"What if I fail again?"* This fear of relapse can be paralysing, whispering that there's no point in trying if we can't guarantee perfection. It convinces us that one misstep will erase all our progress, that slipping back into old habits means we were never truly sincere. But this fear is a deception—it turns repentance into an all-or-nothing pursuit when Tawbah is a lifelong journey, not a one-time event.

The wisdom of our beloved Prophet peace be upon him shines through here:

> *"O people, seek forgiveness, for I seek forgiveness a hundred times a day." (Muslim Hadith 2702)*

If the most beloved to Allah sought forgiveness constantly, what does that tell us about the nature of our faith? This profound advice isn't a call to perfection—it's an encouragement to persist. True Tawbah isn't about never making mistakes again; it's about continuously turning back to Allah, no matter how many times we fall. Every time we seek His forgiveness, we renew our connection with Him, strengthening the very relationship that sin seeks to weaken.

Allah's mercy is not fragile. It doesn't waver based on our failures. It is vast, unshakable, and endlessly patient. No matter how often we return, each moment of sincere repentance is welcomed. So, rather than fearing failure, we should embrace the beauty of beginning again, knowing that Allah never tires of forgiving as long as we never tire of seeking Him.

Silencing the Doubts and Embracing the Journey

It's time to quiet those lingering doubts that hold you back, making you question if you're even worthy of repentance. It's time to confront the harsh whispers of your nafs, the self-doubt that weighs heavy on your heart, and the cunning tricks of Shaytan, who thrives on keeping you distant from Allah's mercy. Tawbah is not a privilege reserved for the pious; it is an open door for everyone, no matter how far we feel we've strayed.

But how do we walk through that door? How do we take Tawbah from a vague concept to a daily practice that nourishes our hearts? The answer lies in a simple but profound roadmap—four practical steps that will anchor you in returning to Allah. These steps are not theoretical ideals; they are tried and tested, grounded in the wisdom of our faith and the lived experiences of those who have walked this path before.

As a special gift, I'm excited to share my favourite step with you—a hidden gem that has illuminated my heart in my darkest moments. This practice has kept me grounded, even when I stumbled, offering a lifeline when I needed it most. Are you ready to take that first step? Let's begin.

Step 1: The Whispered Repentance

Before you sleep, take a moment in solitude. Whisper your regrets to Allah, not in fear, but in hope. Say:

"Ya Allah, I have wronged myself, but Your mercy is greater than my sins. Draw me back to You."

Let this be the last thing your heart clings to before sleep

A Detour to Jannah

overtakes you.

Step 2: The Gratitude Exchange

For every sin you regret, balance it with gratitude. Instead of dwelling in guilt, pause and say: *" Ya Allah, despite my shortcomings, You still bless me with [name a blessing]. Help me turn back to You."*

This shift reframes Tawbah as an act of love rather than punishment.

Step 3: The Silent Companion

Carry a small stone, a bracelet, or a misbaha (prayer beads) as a tangible reminder of your intention to change. Each time you hold it, make a silent Istighfar:

"Astaghfirullah wa atubu ilayh."

Let it ground you in moments of weakness.

Step 4: The Renewal Ritual

When guilt feels heavy, make wudu with purpose. As water flows over your hands, imagine your sins being washed away. Say: *"O Allah, cleanse my heart as You cleanse my limbs."*

Follow with two rak'ahs of sincere repentance, letting each prostration bring you closer to Him.

Bonus Exercise:

1. Write a letter to your guilt:

> *"Dear Shame, you convinced me I was too broken to return. But today, I choose Allah's mercy over your lies."*

2. Tear it up and throw it away.

Tawbah isn't about erasing your past but reclaiming your future. Every *"Astaghfirullah"* is a step out of the wilderness. Every tear is a prayer. Every relapse is a chance to rediscover Allah's patience.

In sharing these reflections, I invite you to see Tawbah not as a daunting leap but as a series of gentle, daily returns to Allah's mercy and love. Embrace each step as a part of your journey, knowing that every moment of sincere repentance draws you nearer to the One who loves you unconditionally.

Let's silence the doubts, overcome our inner struggles, and march steadily toward the light that always awaits us.

> *"Ya Allah, I'm turning to You today—not because I'm strong, but because You are. Forgive, heal, and let my tawbah become a story of Your mercy. Ameen."*

CHAPTER FIVE
FINDING YOUR NORTH STAR

In the darkest night, the stars begin to appear—not all at once, but one by one, timid at first, then bolder until the entire sky is ablaze with light. It's a quiet miracle, unfolding in slow motion, as if the universe is whispering a promise: Even here, in the deepest dark, light will find you. For the believer, that light is Rahma—the infinite mercy of Allah.

The North Star never fades. It remains steady in a world of shifting constellations, unshaken by storms, unchanged by time. It is the celestial reminder that you are never truly lost, no matter how far you have wandered. Even when your feet are unsteady and the road behind you is littered with missteps, the path home remains open, waiting only for you to take the first step.

You know the silence after the storm—the kind that presses against your chest, thick with unshed tears and unspoken regrets. A stillness so heavy it feels like the world itself is holding its breath. *I know this silence.*

The first time I felt the weight of Allah's mercy, not as a concept, but as something real—something alive. It was a night much like any other, except it wasn't. The air in the room was still, the walls closing in with the weight of my thoughts. I sat on the edge of my bed, my heart heavy, my hands limp in my lap, my mind tangled in questions I did not have answers to. *How did I get here?* I whispered into the emptiness. *How do I find my way back?*

And then, like a whisper carried by the wind, the answer settled in my chest:

"You don't have to find your way back. I am already here."

It wasn't a voice. Not exactly. It was a presence, a warmth that unfurled within me, wrapping itself around the ache in my soul. A certainty that defied logic. A love that had been waiting all along.

At that moment, I understood something I had always known but never truly grasped: **Allah's mercy is not something you earn. It's not something you deserve. It's something you are.**

It is the breath in your lungs, the beat of your heart, the unspoken forgiveness in every dawn. The unseen hand steadies you when you stumble, the quiet reassurance in the verses that find you when you need them most. The light never stops shining, even when your eyes are closed.

And when you are ready to open them, to lift your gaze from the ground, to take that first trembling step—**you will find Him waiting.** You always have.

This chapter is about that light. Here, you will learn:

- What *Rahma* truly means is beyond mercy, toward unconditional love.
- Stories of those who found their way back through Allah's mercy.
- Practical steps to make *Rahma* a daily practice, not a distant hope.

Mercy is not a passive whisper; it is the breath of Allah that stirs the universe into motion. It is the force that cradles galaxies and mends shattered hearts with the same infinite care. To understand *Rahma*—divine mercy—is to recognise it as the very fabric of existence, woven into every sunrise, every heartbeat, and every tear that falls in the quiet of the night.

Ar-Rahman: The Mercy That Holds the Universe

Allah's name, **Ar-Rahman**, is more than just a title—it is a cosmic embrace, an all-encompassing mercy that blankets every living soul, believer and non-believer alike. It is the gentle breath of the morning breeze, the rhythmic rise and fall of the ocean, and the quiet comfort in a child's laughter.

The rain quenches barren land, reviving earth that had long surrendered to drought. It is how a wounded heart still dares to hope, how the sun continues rising even after the darkest night. The instinctive love a mother feels for her child, fierce and unwavering, reflects the divine care that nurtures all of existence.

This mercy is woven into the fabric of the universe, an unspoken promise that no matter how lost we feel, there is always a way back. It is in the forgiveness we give and receive, in the moments of peace that come when we least expect them. It is in the food that nourishes us, the water that sustains us, the unseen protection from harm that we will never fully comprehend.

Ar-Raheem: The Mercy That Knows Your Name

If **Ar-Rahman** is Allah's vast, all-encompassing mercy that touches all of creation, then **Ar-Raheem** is mercy turned intimate—a love so personal it feels like a secret between you and Allah. The quiet, unseen tenderness meets you exactly where you are, wrapping around your heart like a familiar embrace.

Ar-Raheem is the forgiveness that finds you in your darkest hour, not waiting for you to be worthy, but embracing you simply because you are His. It is the unexpected solace that cradles you when grief suffocates, the inexplicable peace that settles your soul when you thought you would never breathe freely again. It is the moment of relief after a whispered du'a, the sudden clarity after days of confusion, the lightness in your chest when you thought your burdens would break you.

Ar-Raheem is the quiet voice that whispers, **"I am here"** when you've forgotten how to pray, when your hands tremble with hesitation, when words fail you, and all you can offer are silent tears. It is the unseen hand that lifts you when you stumble, the mercy that stays with you even when you feel unworthy, the patience of a Lord who never turns away—even when you do.

His mercy is not distant, nor is it reserved for the perfect. It is near, tender, and deeply personal. It is the reminder that no matter how far you have strayed, **Allah's love has never left you.**

In the Japanese art of *kintsugi*, broken pottery is repaired with gold, not to hide the cracks but to celebrate them. The flaws become part of the pottery's story, and its brokenness magnifies its beauty. You are that vessel. Your mistakes, regrets, and heartaches are not flaws to erase—they are fissures where Allah's mercy pours in, gilding your pain with purpose. Whenever you think, *"I am too broken,"* remember: Allah does not love you *despite* your cracks. He loves you *because* of them. They are the spaces where His light enters.

The Prophet peace be upon him said:

> *"By Him in whose hand is my soul, if you were not to sin, Allah would replace you with a people who would sin and then seek forgiveness from Allah, and He would forgive them."*

> *(Sahih Muslim 2749)*

Even in suffering, mercy is the thread stitching your story together. Allah's mercy is not the absence of pain—it is the courage to rise *through* it and the resilience to bloom *because* of it. It is the promise that no tear is wasted, no prayer unheard, and no soul beyond repair.

Allah says in the Quran:

> *"When those who believe in Our verses come*
> *to you, say, 'Peace be upon you. Your Lord*
> *has decreed upon Himself mercy: that any of*
> *you who does wrong out of ignorance and*
> *then repents after that and corrects himself—*
> *indeed, He is Forgiving and Merciful."*
> *(Surah Al-An'am 6:54)*

Would you believe me if I told you that Allah's mercy seeks you out relentlessly, like the tide returning to shore?

The Prophet peace be on him said:

> *"Allah is more merciful to His servants than*
> *a mother is to her child." (Bukhari Hadith*
> *10)*

Imagine a mother searching for her lost child during a raging storm. She pushes through the wind, calling their name over and over, her voice breaking with each cry. She does not stop—she cannot stop because love like that knows no surrender.

Now multiply that love infinitely. That is Allah's pursuit of you. No matter how far you've strayed or how lost you feel, His mercy is already racing towards you, calling you back home. It is not passive or conditional. It does not wait for you to be "good enough." It follows you into your darkest moments, knocking gently at the door of your heart, whispering: *Return to Me, for I have never left you.*

The Story of the Runaway

Khalid was once a bright and joyful boy, full of hope and dreams for his future. But as the years passed, he found himself drifting further away from the faith that had once been a guiding light in his life. The world around him seemed full of temptations and distractions, and he began to lose himself in them. He stopped praying, made choices that pulled him farther from Allah, and questioned the very existence of His mercy. His heart grew heavy, and the guilt of his actions weighed him down, but he didn't know how to return.

His mother, a woman of deep faith, could see the changes in her son. She watched with quiet sorrow as Khalid grew distant and lost his connection to Allah. Night after night, while Khalid lay in his bed, his mother would stand in the quiet of the night, raising her hands in prayer, pleading with Allah to guide her son back. *"Ya Allah, please bring my Khalid back to You,"* she would whisper through tear-filled eyes. *"Forgive him, guide his heart, and show him the way."*

Despite his mother's constant prayers, Khalid continued walking down a path that felt darker each day. Yet, his mother's love never wavered. Every prayer was a silent plea for mercy, every moment spent in supplication an act of love that never gave up. She knew that Allah's mercy was greater than anything her son had done and believed

Khalid would return to Him one day.

One evening, Khalid was out with friends, far from the warmth of his home. He felt the emptiness inside him more than ever, and as he looked up at the sky, he couldn't help but wonder, Is this really all there is? He had everything he thought he wanted, but something was missing—a deep, aching void that nothing could fill. Then, something stirred inside him—a faint whisper that seemed to come from within his soul, reminding him of his mother's words: *"Don't forget Allah. He is always there for you."*

The next day, Khalid returned home to find his mother sitting in prayer. Her peaceful face, hands raised to the sky, filled his heart with a warmth he hadn't felt in so long. As he watched his mother, something shifted in Khalid's heart. The anger and confusion he had carried for so long began to dissolve. He realised that, despite everything, his mother had never given up on him. His mother's constant prayers and unwavering faith were a beacon of light waiting for him to return.

That night, Khalid found himself on his knees, praying for the first time in years. He didn't know where to start, but his heart was full of gratitude and remorse. He whispered, *"Ya Allah, forgive me. I have strayed so far, but you are always there to guide me back."*

As tears flowed, he felt a peace wash over him—an undeniable feeling that Allah's mercy was real and there for him, no matter how lost he had felt. In that moment, Khalid understood the power of his mother's prayers. His mother's faith had carried him through the darkest times, and Allah's mercy had brought him back.

A Mercy that knows no Bounds

One of my favourite space stories (also the only one I know) that beautifully captures the vastness of Allah's mercy is the story of Sheikh Muszaphar Shukor, a Malaysian astronaut who in 2007 became the first Muslim to journey into space during Ramadan. As he floated 200 miles above the Earth, suspended in the infinite expanse of the universe, he looked out at the vastness of space—an awe-inspiring sight of endless stars, planets, and galaxies. In that moment, he felt a deep connection to Allah, and with profound humility, he opened a Quran and began to pray:

"Ya Allah, in this vastness, I see Your mercy. Even here, You are near."

To think that Allah's mercy, which stretches across the unimaginable reaches of the universe, can also fill the smallest corners of our hearts is nothing short of miraculous. If Allah's mercy can encompass the entire universe, then no part of you—no matter how broken or distant you may feel—is beyond His reach. His mercy has no limits. It is not bound by time or space. It is present in every breath you take, every heartbeat, and even moments of despair. Just as Sheikh Muszaphar felt Allah's presence in the vastness of space, know that no matter where you are or how far you may feel from Him, His mercy is always near, waiting to embrace you.

Let's take a moment to reflect on the countless blessings and moments of mercy that weave through our lives, often unnoticed. In the hustle of daily life, we may forget to pause and acknowledge how Allah's mercy manifests in the smallest gestures, the quiet moments, and even in our struggles. So, let's open our hearts and journals and begin to capture the mercy surrounding us—reminding ourselves that no matter how distant we may feel, we are always held in Allah's loving embrace.

Day 1-3: Each night, write one way Allah showed you mercy that day.   *"A stranger paid for my coffee"I survived the panic attack."*

Day 4-7: Reflect on past hardships. Write:

"This pain taught me ...."

"Allah's mercy showed up through..........."

Day 8: Write a letter to Allah:

"Ya Rahman, I used to think You were far away. Now I see You in..........."

"Ya Ar-Rahman, When I am lost, be my compass. When I am broken, be my glue. When I forget my name, remind me I am Yours. Let Your mercy be the North Star I turn to When the world goes dark—Not because I deserve it, But because You promised it. Ameen

CHAPTER SIX
OVERCOMING
SHAME & GUILT

Shame is a silent architect, slowly building walls around the heart, brick by brick, using memories of past mistakes, whispers of inadequacy, and the weight of *"what if."* It convinces us that we are defined by our actions and that the person we once were, is the person we will always be.

A sister once shared a story with me that made my heart ache. She said: *"I remember a time when my walls felt insurmountable. It was a cold evening, and I stood outside a mosque, unsure whether I should enter. I hadn't prayed in so long, and the guilt of abandoning my faith weighed down on me like a heavy cloak. I felt like I was doomed anyway, like my sins were too great to be forgiven, so why even try? I was afraid that if I stepped inside, my sins would somehow pollute the sacred space. I stood there, paralysed, too ashamed to move."*

It was then that a friend appeared, noticing her hesitation. She walked up to her with a gentle smile, offering a wordless invitation to come inside. Her presence was calming, as though she could sense the turmoil in her heart. They sat in the back, and the friend spoke softly as if she could read her mind:

"Shame can make us believe we don't deserve Allah's mercy," she said. *"But His mercy is never far from us, even when we feel most distant."*

Her words pierced the sister's heart, and she realised she wasn't alone. Allah's mercy isn't something we earn or deserve based on how "good" we've been—it's a gift, always waiting for us. She understood that guilt is tied to actions, but shame distorts who we believe we are. It tells us we are unworthy, undeserving of Allah's love and mercy.

That night, she stood before Allah, not with perfect prayers, but with a heart full of yearning for His forgiveness. Through her tears, she whispered, *"Ya Allah, forgive me. Take away my shame and replace it with Your mercy."*

At that moment, she felt a peace she hadn't known in years. The walls she had built around her heart—constructed by shame—began to crumble. She realised that her past didn't define her; Allah's mercy did. And with each tear that fell, she felt His mercy enveloping her, reminding her that no matter how far she had strayed, the door to His forgiveness was always open.

This chapter isn't about erasing your past, but about understanding that your past doesn't have the power to keep you away from Allah. His mercy is always greater than any wall of shame we've built around ourselves.

Understanding the Roots: Guilt vs. Shame

Guilt whispers: *"I did something wrong."* The quiet voice rises when we've made a mistake, urging us to reflect on our actions and make amends. Guilt has the potential to be a teacher, a momentary reminder that we can do better and be better. It calls us to repentance, to return to the straight path, and to seek forgiveness from Allah. Guilt, when acknowledged and processed, becomes a tool for growth. The nudge reminds us that we are not perfect, but that doesn't mean we can't change.

Shame, however, hisses: *"I am wrong."* It goes beyond what we've done and penetrates the core of who we think we are. Shame convinces us that our mistakes define our entire being and that our wrongdoings permanently stain our character. It whispers lies that we are inherently flawed, that we will always be unworthy, unlovable, and undeserving of Allah's mercy.

Guilt is a call to action—it asks us to repent, to make things right, and to strive to do better. It reminds us that we are capable of change and that our past does not have to dictate our future. But shame, shame is a prison warden. It locks us in a cell of self-doubt and self-loathing, convincing us that we are unworthy of freedom. Shame tells us that we are beyond redemption, that we have no place in Allah's mercy, and that we don't deserve the chance to heal.

Where guilt can lead to redemption, shame often leads to isolation. It can make us turn away from Allah, thinking that we have strayed too far to return and that the doors of forgiveness are closed to us. But Allah's mercy is vast, and no matter how deep the shame feels, it is never stronger than His willingness to forgive.

This is why it's so important to differentiate between the two. We should learn from our guilt, but we must reject shame. Allah has promised that no matter how far we've fallen, He is always ready to guide us back. Our mistakes don't define us; they are simply moments we can learn from on our journey back to Him.

The Science of Shame:

Neuroscientists have found that shame activates the brain's pain centres, triggering neural responses similar to those experienced during physical injury. This means that the emotional pain of shame can feel just as intense as physical harm. When we experience shame, our brain processes it like a physical wound, intensifying our sense of emotional distress and discomfort. This biological response helps explain why shame feels so deeply painful and can be so difficult to shake off. It's as if our very sense of self is under attack, and this deep-seated pain can linger, affecting our mental and emotional well-being for long periods of time.

Unlike guilt, which is focused on a specific behaviour or action, shame is more insidious because it attacks our sense of self-worth. While guilt says, *"I did something wrong,"* shame says, *"I am wrong."* Guilt can lead to positive change and growth because it helps us reflect on and correct our actions. But shame corrodes our sense of value, making us believe that we are inherently flawed, unworthy of love, and undeserving of forgiveness. This deep-rooted feeling of unworthiness can create a vicious cycle, where the more we feel ashamed of ourselves, the more we withdraw from others and Allah's mercy.

An Islamic Lens:

The Quran acknowledges human fallibility but never equates sin with identity, consistently reminding us that our actions do not define who we are in the eyes of Allah.

One powerful example of this distinction is found in the verse:

> *"Say, 'O My servants who have harmed yourselves by your own actions, do not despair of Allah's mercy. Indeed, Allah forgives all sins. Indeed, it is He who is the Forgiving, the Merciful." (Surah Az- Zumar 39:53)*

In this verse, Allah invites us to never lose hope in His boundless mercy despite our shortcomings and transgressions. He directly separates the action from the individual, emphasising that no matter what we have done wrong, it does not define our worth in His eyes.

Allah does not see us through the lens of our mistakes; instead, He sees us as His servants, capable of turning back to Him in repentance. Sin is a separate entity, not the essence of who we are. Allah's message here is clear:

Regardless of how lost we may feel, the path to forgiveness is never closed. All it takes is to approach Him with a sincere heart and humility.

The Journey Back to Your True Self

The Prophet peace be upon him said:

> *"Allah stretches out His hand at night to forgive those who have sinned by day, and He stretches out His hand by day to forgive those who have sinned by night—until the sun rises from the west." (Muslim Hadith 2429)*

Tawbah is not simply a transactional eraser of sins—it's a pilgrimage of the soul. It's the journey of moving beyond guilt and shame and rediscovering who you are in the eyes of Allah. Here's how to walk this path:

1. Acknowledge: The Courage to Name the Wound

- **Guilt** says, "I did this. I own it." It's the honest confrontation with your actions, without sugarcoating or blame-shifting.
- **Shame**, on the other hand, whispers, "I am this. I am unworthy." It convinces you that your mistakes define who you are, chaining you to the past.

Example: When the Companion Ka'b ibn Malik (R.A) missed the Battle of Tabuk, he did not justify his absence. He stood before the Prophet peace be upon him and said: "I stayed behind with no excuse."

95

(Bukhari Hadith 4419) He owned his actions without letting shame convince him he was beyond redemption.

2. Regret: The Sacred Ache

- **Guilt** is about feeling the weight of your actions, yet it moves you toward growth and change. It's the realisation that you want to do better.
- **Shame**, however, paralyses you. It's the feeling of being broken, worthless, and beyond repair.

Rather than wallowing in shame, let the **regret** be a **sacred ache**—the grief for the distance your choices created between you and Allah. Like a parent mourning a lost child, feel the loss of connection, but do not let that grief keep you from returning to Him.

3. Commit: The Bridge Between Words and Action

- **Guilt** calls for repentance, for action that follows the remorse.
- **Shame** causes us to believe we are too far gone to make any change.

Replace empty promises with one tangible step. If gossip is your struggle, text a friend: "Hold me accountable—if I backbite, redirect me." Act on your regret and let it push you toward transformation. The journey back to your true self requires tangible steps to break the cycle of shame and embrace the mercy of Allah.

The Girl Who Reclaimed Her Name

A Detour to Jannah

Zahra was raised in a family where faith was the cornerstone of life, but during her time at university, she became swept up in a lifestyle of parties and fleeting pleasures. She pushed Islam to the back of her mind, seeking validation in all the wrong places. Years later, she found herself in a rehab centre, her body weakened by years of self-destruction and her heart feeling empty and disconnected from everything she once held dear.

One night, in a moment of deep reflection, she vividly dreamed of her late father reciting a verse from Surah Ar-Rum: *"So direct your face toward the religion, inclining to truth"* (30:30). His voice, filled with love and guidance, pierced through the darkness she had been living in. It felt like a call to return to the truth she had abandoned.

Desperate for change, Zahra emailed her local mosque, asking, "I don't know how to pray anymore. Can someone teach me?" The Imam responded gently and welcomingly: *"Come as you are. We'll learn together."*

Zahra's return to faith reflects the three crucial steps of Tawbah:

- **Acknowledge***: "I abandoned my faith in search of temporary pleasures, and in doing so, I lost my peace."*
- **Regret:** *"I mourn the years I spent chasing distractions instead of nurturing my relationship with Allah."*

- **Commit:** She began attending a weekly support group for recovering individuals at the mosque, seeking spiritual healing and accountability.

Through this process, Layla's journey reminds us that no matter how far we stray, the door to return to Allah remains wide open.

Exercise: The Mercy Mirror

1. Stand before a mirror and say: *"Allah created me. He knows my flaws and loves me still."*
2. Repeat daily until your reflection reminds you of divine love, not imperfection.

Rewriting the Narrative

This involves shifting the way we view ourselves, our past, and our relationship with Allah. Instead of seeing our mistakes and shortcomings as defining who we are, we can see them as opportunities for growth, learning, and the extension of Allah's mercy. This is a conscious effort to let go of the negative labels that shame places on us and to rewrite the story of who we are in light of Allah's infinite mercy and forgiveness.

Here's how to do it:

- **Recognise the Old Story:**

First, identify the narrative that shame has written for

you. Perhaps it's one of being unworthy, hopeless, or forever bound by your past actions. Acknowledge these feelings without letting them define your future.

- **Challenge the Lies of Shame:**

Shame often whispers, *"You are broken beyond repair."* But the Quran reminds us of Allah's mercy, greater than any sin. When shame tells you you are unworthy, challenge it with the truth of Allah's forgiveness and the belief that you are never too far from His mercy.

- **Embrace the New Narrative:**

Begin to replace the story of shame with a narrative of hope, growth, and redemption. Your past does not define you; your willingness to turn back to Allah does. You are a servant of the Most Merciful, capable of change and transformation. Just as a story has chapters, your life is unfolding, and each chapter is an opportunity to rewrite your path.

- **Speak Words of Mercy:**

Your words have power. Instead of speaking to yourself with condemnation, speak words of self-compassion, understanding, and mercy. This doesn't mean excusing mistakes but acknowledging your humanity and your ability to return to Allah in repentance.

- **Act in Alignment with the New Story:**

Your actions reflect the story you tell yourself. If you

believe you are worthy of Allah's mercy, you will act with the intention to improve and seek nearness to Him. Engage in acts of worship, seek knowledge, and surround yourself with those who uplift you in your journey.

From Self-Loathing to Self-Compassion

The Prophet peace be upon him taught:

> *"None of you should say: 'My soul has become evil.' He should say: 'My soul is in bad shape." (Muslim Hadith 2998)*

This profound teaching reminds us that while we may falter, our failures do not define our essence. We can all transform; even in our lowest moments, we are not beyond redemption.

Affirmations Rooted in Faith:

"Allah believes in my capacity to change."
"My worth is defined by His mercy, not my mistakes."

By shifting the focus from self-loathing to self-compassion, we embrace Allah's mercy, acknowledging our flaws without letting them define us. We are always worthy of His love and capable of becoming better with each step we take toward Him.

Exercise: The Forgiveness Timeline

1. Draw a timeline of your life. Mark moments of guilt/shame in red and mercy in gold.
2. Reflect: *"How did Allah's mercy meet me even in the red moments?"*

The Man Who Forgave Himself

After causing a car accident that left a close friend injured, Ahmed found himself overwhelmed with guilt and regret. The weight of his actions became unbearable, and he spiralled into a deep depression. He withdrew from friends, avoided the community, and found it hard to even look at himself in the mirror. Every day, he replayed the accident in his mind, convinced that he could never make up for the pain he had caused.

One day, seeking solace, Ahmed visited a local sheikh who had always been a source of wisdom and guidance. The sheikh listened patiently to his story and offered advice that changed Ahmed's life. *"Allah forgave you the moment you asked for forgiveness,"* the sheikh said. *"Now forgive yourself. It's time to release the burden of guilt you're carrying and trust in Allah's mercy. You cannot undo the past, but you can shape the future."*

A Detour to Jannah

Those words pierced through the darkness in Ahmed's heart. He realised that his failure to forgive himself was keeping him chained to the past, preventing him from moving forward. With renewed clarity, Ahmed understood that true repentance wasn't just about seeking forgiveness from Allah but also about acknowledging the forgiveness He had already granted and accepting that part of healing was to forgive himself.

Ahmed made a decision to act on his renewed understanding. He began volunteering at community centres, offering his time to help those in need. He used his experience and guilt as a source of motivation to give back to others, turning his feelings of regret into a force for good. Each time he helped someone, he felt a sense of redemption. Through service, he found a way to repay the debt of guilt he had carried, not by changing the past, but by changing the way he responded to it.

His work at the community centres allowed him to serve others and helped him rebuild his sense of self-worth. He began to feel connected to the world around him again, and the depression that once consumed him began to loosen its grip. The guilt he had once carried so heavily now felt lighter as he channelled it into acts of kindness and service.

Ahmed's journey of healing became a testament to the power of forgiveness—both divine and self-forgiveness—and the transformative power of service. His life, once defined by a tragic mistake, was now marked by his efforts to make a positive impact on those around him.

The Duas That Disarm Shame

Du'a for Self-Acceptance: "Ya Allah, help me see myself through Your eyes—flawed but worthy, broken but beloved."

Du'a for Release: "Ya Ghaffar, erase the shame that binds me. Replace it with the courage to begin again."

Prophetic Dua: "Allahumma inni as'aluka hubbaka, wa hubba man yuhibbuka, wa hubba 'amalun yuqarribuni ila hubbika."

> *"O Allah, I ask for Your love, the love of those who love You, and deeds that will bring me closer to Your love." (Sunan Ibn Majah, Hadith 1395)*

The Freedom Beyond the Cage

Shame is a fire that burns only what you feed it. Starve it with truth: You are not your mistakes. You are not the worst thing you've done. You are a soul Allah fashioned with purpose, mercy, and the capacity to rise.

The Liberation Letter

1. Write a letter to shame: *"You convinced me I was unworthy. Today, I choose Allah's truth."*
2. Burn it, scatter the ashes, and recite: *"Ya Allah, make my heart a place where mercy dwells, not shame."*

PART THREE:
THE JOURNEY BACK

CHAPTER SEVEN
DETACHING FROM HARMFUL HABITS

You stand at the river's edge, arms trembling under the weight of stones you've carried for years—some pebbles, others boulders. Each one a story: the *habit* you rationalise as harmless, the *relationship* that drains your Iman, the *grudge* fossilised into your ribs. They clatter together— a dissonant symphony of "I'll quit tomorrow," "They need me," and "This is just who I am." The river ahead churns with divine promise, its currents whispering, *"Come home."* But the stones anchor you to the shore of stagnation, their weight familiar, almost comforting.

The Anatomy of Stones

- **The Pebbles**: Seemingly innocent—the Instagram scrolls that steal your Fajr, the Netflix binges that numb your nights. Tiny thieves of time, they pile up until your soul's ledger reads bankrupt.
- **The Boulders**: Crushing, jagged—the toxic friendship mocking your hijab, the addiction you've swaddled in secrecy, the envy rotting your heart. You've lugged them so long; their edges have carved grooves into your palms.

A Detour to Jannah

Allah says,

> *"And whoever turns away from My remembrance—indeed, he will have a depressed life..." (Quran 20:124).*

These stones are not burdens; they are *choices*. Choices to clutch the finite while the Infinite beckons.

The River's Secret

The water isn't calm. It rages with tests, but also with *Tawfiq*—divine enablement. To cross, you must unclench your fists. Every stone sunk becomes a stepping stone, not to walk *on*, but to walk *past*. The Prophet peace be upon him taught:

> *"Be in this world as if you were a stranger or a traveller passing by" (Bukhari).*

Travelers pack lightly.

Imagine the sister wading in, her stones—a toxic job, a boyfriend haram as alcohol—plunging into the depths. The current tugs her hijab, but her hands, now empty, reach for the One who parts seas. Or the brother dropping his stone of pride, feeling his spine straighten not with arrogance, but with the humility of *Sujood*.

The Art of Unclenching

Letting go isn't a one-time purge. It's a daily *jihad*:

1. **Acknowledge the Weight**: *"This scrolling isn't relaxation—it's avoidance."*

2. **Name the Stone**: *"I hold onto this haram relationship because I fear loneliness more than Allah's displeasure."*

3. **Cast It with Intention**: Not a frantic toss, but a release whispered with *"Astaghfirullah"*—a plea for Allah to replace what's lost with what's better.

Allah says:

> *"Perhaps you hate a thing and it is good for you…" (Quran 2:216).*

That stone you dread releasing? It's absence will feel like amputation—until it doesn't. Until you realise the phantom pain was the echo of a cage.

The Currents of Mercy

The river isn't your enemy. Its turbulence is Allah's mercy scrubbing the residue of Dunya from your skin. Each wave that knocks you breathless is a lesson: *"You are not in control, but I AM."*

You'll falter. Old stones will reappear, slick with Shaytan's whispers: *"You need this. You deserve this."* But the Quran's verse will anchor you: *"And whoever relies upon Allah—He will be sufficient for him"* (65:3). Sufficiency isn't abundance—it's liberation from wanting more.

The Far Shore

Imagine the moment your foot touches the other side. The stones? Still there, buried under river silt. But you—you are lighter. Your salah lingers, no longer rushed. Your du'as drip with dependency, not demands. The people who matter find you—not because you chased them, but because you radiate the peace of *Tawakkul.*

Allah's light doesn't demand perfection. It asks for space. Empty your arms, and He will fill them with purpose. The stones were never yours to bear—they were your chains to break.

Take the First Step

Look down. Press that stone in your hand—the one you've named "I can't quit" or "They'll judge me"—to your heart. Then let it fall. Watch the ripples merge with the river's flow. Each release is a declaration: *"Allah is enough."*

The far shore isn't a destination. It's a return—to your *fitrah*, to the self Allah moulded from clay and destined for Jannah. The river? It was never meant to drown you. It was meant to cleanse you.

Cross, beloved traveller. Your Lord waits on the other side, arms wide, stones forgotten.

What's Weighing You Down?

Habits That Drain Your Spirit

Social Media Obsession: Hours spent mindlessly scrolling through feeds or binge-watching videos can rob you of precious time—time that could be devoted to reciting the Qur'an, performing your salah, or engaging in dhikr. These digital distractions often leave you empty and disconnected from your inner peace.

Irregular Spiritual Practices: Perhaps you only engage in worship during the month of Ramadan or on special occasions. Skipping daily prayers or neglecting consistent dhikr can create a gap between your heart and your Creator, weakening the connection that sustains your soul.

Unhealthy Escapism: Instead of addressing the underlying pain or stress in your life, you might turn to overeating, excessive television, or other indulgences. These coping mechanisms offer temporary relief but numb your spirit in the long run rather than allowing proper healing to begin.

Toxic Influences

Friends Who Diminish Your Faith: It can be painful when friends or colleagues make light of your commitment, questioning your choices with remarks like, "Why do you always have to be so serious about your beliefs?" Such comments can sow seeds of doubt and make you feel isolated.

Family Expectations: Sometimes, those closest to us pressure us to conform to their vision of normalcy. Phrases like "You need to relax and not take everything so seriously" can be well-meaning yet dismissive of the profound commitment you're trying to nurture. This familial pressure can force you to compromise on your values.

Work Cultures That Clash with Your Values: Ethical

compromises are common and celebrated in some professional environments. However, when colleagues normalise practices that conflict with one's understanding of halal living or when one's workplace dismisses spiritual pursuits as irrelevant, it becomes challenging to maintain one's inner balance.

Environments That Stifle Growth

Disorganised Surroundings: Your physical space is a mirror of your inner world. A cluttered or chaotic environment can contribute to mental and spiritual disarray, making it harder to find moments of calm and reflection. Whether it's your home or workspace, an unorganised area can be a constant reminder of unresolved clutter within your mind.

Media That Erodes Values: The content you consume shapes your perceptions and beliefs. If you're frequently exposed to music, movies, or literature glorifying materialism, unethical behaviour, or trivial pursuits, it can subtly erode your values. Over time, these influences can shift your focus away from what truly matters.

The Stone Inventory

Take a moment to inventory the stones you're carrying. This exercise is a step toward understanding what weighs you down and recognising the growth potential that awaits you once you release these burdens.

List Three Stones:
Identify three habits, influences, or environments that drain your spiritual energy. These might be as subtle as a recurring distraction or as pronounced as a toxic relationship.

Reflect on Their Cost:
For each stone, ask yourself:

- "What is this costing me regarding my spiritual well-being and peace of mind?"

- "What could I gain by letting this go and making room for Allah's light?"

By honestly assessing these stones, you will begin to see that every burden you release is an act of self-love—a way of stepping closer to the vibrant life that Allah has envisioned for you. Each stone left behind promises renewed freedom and spiritual fulfilment waiting on the other side of the river.

The Art Of Letting Go

Start Small: The 1% Rule

Example: If social media consumes 3 hours daily, reduce it by 1% (about 2 minutes). Gradually increase this over weeks.

Why It Works: Small changes are sustainable and build

momentum.

Replace, Don't Erase

Swap Harmful Habits: Replace binge-watching with Quran recitation or a podcast on Islamic history.

Example: Instead of gossiping, say: *"Let's make dua for them instead."*

Set Boundaries with Toxic Influences

Scripts for Tough Conversations:

"I love you but I must prioritise my faith now."

"I'm not comfortable with this—let's find something else to do."

When to Walk Away: If someone consistently undermines your values, distance yourself with kindness

---

Create a Sacred Space

Declutter Your Environment: A clean, organised space fosters clarity and peace.

Designate a Prayer Corner: Even a small mat and a Quran can transform a corner into a sanctuary.

The Power of Accountability

Find a Tawbah Buddy: Someone who shares your goals and checks in weekly.

Example: *"This week, I'll cut my screen time by 10%. Can you hold me to it?"*

Stories Of Breaking Free

The Social Media Detox

Maryam was a self-proclaimed Instagram addict. She spent hours scrolling through perfectly curated feeds, comparing her life to the highlight reels of others. *"I'd see friends travelling, getting married, or landing dream jobs, and I'd feel like I was falling behind,"* she shared.

One Ramadan, during a particularly emotional Taraweeh prayer, she realised: *"I'm giving my time and energy to strangers online while my connection with Allah is fading."* That night, she deleted the app.

The first week was tough. *"I kept reaching for my phone out of habit,"* she admitted. *"I felt FOMO— fear of missing out—on everything."* But as the days passed, something shifted. *"I started noticing the beauty around me— the way the sunlight filtered through my window, the sound of birds in* the morning. I had more time for the Quran, my family, and myself."

Maryam's story is a testament to the *joy of missing out*—on negativity, comparison, and wasted time. *"I didn't lose anything by leaving social media,"* she said. *"I gained my life back."*

The Brother Who Left the Haram Job

Yusuf worked as a bartender for years, serving alcohol to numb his pain. *"I hated it,"* he confessed. *"But the money was good, and I didn't know how to leave."*

One night, after serving a drunk patron who broke down in tears, Yusuf had an epiphany: *"I'm contributing to people's destruction. How can I ask Allah for mercy when I'm part of the problem?"*

The next day, he quit. *"I had no backup plan, no savings,"* he said. *"But I trusted Allah would provide."*

Within weeks, a friend connected him with a halal startup looking for someone with his skills. *"The pay was less, but the peace was priceless,"* Yusuf shared. *"Now, I wake up knowing my work aligns with my values. Allah didn't just replace my income—He replaced my shame with dignity."*

The Sister Who Reclaimed Her Time

Noor's evenings were predictable: dinner, dishes, then hours of Netflix. *"I'd tell myself I deserved to unwind,"* she said. *"But deep down, I knew I was* avoiding something—my Quran."

One night, after binge-watching a series that left her feeling empty, she decided to try something new. *"I opened Surah Al-Kahf and set a timer for 30 minutes. I thought I'd hate it, but I was hooked."*

The stories of the People of the Cave, Dhul-Qarnayn, and Musa (AS) captivated her. *"It was better than any show,"* she laughed. *"I started looking forward to my 'Quran time' every night."*

Over time, Noor memorised the entire surah. *"It wasn't just about the words,"* she explained. *"It was about the connection. Allah was speaking directly to me, guiding me through my struggles."*

Noor's story reminds us that when we replace harmful habits with acts of worship, we don't just lose something—we gain everything.

The Duas for Detachment

Du'a for Strength: "Ya Allah, help me let go of what harms me and hold on to what brings me closer to You."

Du'a for Clarity: "Ya Basir (The All-Seeing), show me what I need to release and what I need to embrace."

The Freedom of Release

Letting go is not about loss—it's about liberation. Every habit you release, every toxic influence you distance yourself from, every cluttered space you clear creates room for Allah's light to enter.

The Prophet peace be upon him said:

> *"Whoever leaves something for the sake of Allah, Allah will give him something better."(Musnad Ahmad Hadith 20739)*

Now is the moment to release those burdens—the three stones you've identified earlier. Each one has weighed you down, holding you back from the lightness of renewal. But you don't have to carry them anymore. The river before you is flowing, ready to wash them away. Let this be the moment you loosen your grip and step forward, unburdened and free.

The River Crossing Visualisation

- Close your eyes and imagine standing at the river's edge, stones in hand.
- Drop them into the water one by one, saying: *"I release _____ to make space for _____."*
- Step into the river, feeling lighter with each step.

CHAPTER EIGHT
REBUILDING YOUR CONNECTION WITH ALLAH

You are standing at the ruins of a construction site—the heart. Once, it was a sanctuary: walls of gratitude, pillars of prayer, a roof of remembrance sheltering you from life's storms. But time and neglect have left cracks in the foundation. Missed prayers erode the mortar. Distractions chip at the windows. The Qur'an, your blueprint, lies buried under the rubble of busyness. The call to rebuild feels daunting, but Allah—the Ultimate Architect—has already provided the tools, the materials, and the promise:

> *"So remember Me; I will remember you" (Qur'an 2:152).*

The Foundation: Tawheed

Every lasting structure begins with a solid base. Tawheed—the oneness of Allah—is the bedrock. Without it, the house of the heart collapses under the weight of doubt, fear, or worldly attachment. The Prophet peace be upon him said:

> *"Faith has seventy-odd branches, the highest of which is the declaration that none has the right to be worshipped but*

Allah... " *(Bukhari).*

Cracks in the Foundation:

- *Neglect*: Letting career, relationships, or self-doubt become the center of your life.

- *Shirk Subtlety*: Seeking validation from creation over the Creator, fearing people's opinions more than Allah's.

Repair Kit: Return to *La ilaha illallah*. Rebuild your foundation by recentering every brick of your life on His lordship.

The Bricks: Small, Consistent Acts

A house isn't built in a day. Each brick—a Fajr prayer, a verse of Qur'an, a moment of gratitude—is a deliberate choice. The Prophet peace be upon him said:

> *"The most beloved deeds to Allah are those done consistently, even if small" (Bukhari).*

Examples:

- **Salah**: Five daily bricks to reinforce the walls against chaos.

- **Du'a**: Mortar between the bricks, binding your struggles to His mercy.

- **Qur'an**: The blueprint, guiding each brick's placement.

"But I keep failing!" you say. So did the Companions. They built Islam brick by brick, day by day, through persecution and doubt. Your bricks need not be perfect—only sincere.

The Scaffolding: Community

No builder works alone. The ummah is your scaffolding—those who steady you when your walls tremble. The Prophet ﷺ said, *"A believer to another believer is like a building whose different parts enforce each other"* (Bukhari).

Dangers of Isolation:

- Caving to despair: *"No one understands my struggles."*

- Normalising neglect: *"Everyone else is too busy for Allah too."*

Rebuild Together: Attend the masjid, join a halaqa, or text a friend an ayah. Scaffolding is temporary—it's removed once the structure stands firm—but until then, lean on the believers.

The Tools: Mercy and Repentance

Allah doesn't demand a flawless build. He asks for effort. His mercy is the toolbox:

- **Tawbah (Repentance)**: Sandpaper to smooth mistakes.

- **Sabr (Patience)**: A level to steady your progress.

- **Tawakkul (Trust)**: The safety net when fear of failure paralyses you.

The Qur'an says:

> *"O My servants who have transgressed against themselves, do not despair of Allah's mercy. Indeed, Allah forgives all sins" (39:53).*

Every crack repaired with Tawbah becomes a testament to His grace.

The Architect's Promise

You are not the builder—Allah is. Your role is to show up, brick in hand, and trust His design. *"And whoever relies upon Allah—He will be sufficient for him"* (65:3).

When the Storm Hits:

- *Doubt: "Will this ever get easier?"*

- *Setbacks: "I missed Salah again."*

Allah's response:

> *"And We will surely test you with something*
> *of fear and hunger and loss... But give good*
> *tidings to the patient" (2:155).*

Storms reveal weak points, not to destroy you, but to guide your repairs.

The Blueprint: Sunnah

The Prophet peace be upon him is your foreman. His Sunnah is the perfect blueprint:

- **Simplicity**: He prayed on a mat, not a palace.

- **Consistency**: He smiled at a child, forgave an enemy, and stood in prayer until his feet swelled.

- **Balance**: He mended his shoes, joked with his family, and still built a legacy that shakes the world.

You need not erect a skyscraper. Build a *home*—a heart where Allah dwells, where worship is warmth, and every brick radiates love.

The Invitation: Lay Your First Brick

The rubble of guilt is not your identity. The dust of neglect is not your destiny. Today, lay one brick:

- **Pray** one Salah with presence.

- **Read** one Ayah—then reread it, as if Allah wrote it just for you.

- **Whisper** one Du'a from the rubble: *"Ya Allah, help me rebuild."*

Allah says, *"Take one step toward Me, I will take ten steps toward you. Walk to Me, I will run to you"* (Hadith Qudsi). The house of your heart may take a lifetime to perfect, but His mercy is the cement that holds every brick together. Start now. Build again

Embracing Salah

Salah is not merely a ritual but the heartbeat of a believer's life. Each time you stand before Allah in prayer, you can turn inward and rediscover your purpose.

Intentional Moments: Begin by setting aside distractions. Whether it's the quiet of early morning or a peaceful pause in the evening, approach Salah with a clear intention. Let each prayer be a deliberate moment to reconnect with your Creator.

Mindful Presence: As you perform your prayers, focus on each word and movement. Picture the flow of your actions as a conversation—a dialogue where you share your deepest thoughts and listen for Allah's guidance. Even if your mind wanders, gently bring it back to the present moment, knowing each effort counts.

Building Consistency: If your routine has become mechanical, try incorporating small changes. Perhaps extend your time in prostration, allowing more space for reflection, or recite additional verses quietly after the obligatory prayers. Over time, these modest adjustments can transform your connection into a profoundly personal experience.

Speaking Through Du'a: Du'a is your direct line to Allah—a sacred moment where you can be completely honest, vulnerable, and authentic. It is more than just a request; it is an intimate conversation with the One who knows your struggles, hears your unspoken words, and understands the depths of your heart. In Du'a, there is no need for pretense, no fear of judgment—only a space where you can lay down your worries, hopes, and dreams before the One closer to you than your jugular vein.

It's not just about asking for things; it's about connection. It's about turning to Him in gratitude when your heart is full and seeking His comfort when you feel lost. It's about whispering *Alhamdulillah* in moments of joy and *Ya Allah, help me* in times of hardship. It's about lifting your hands, not just in need, but in surrender, acknowledging that every blessing and every challenge is part of His divine wisdom.

In Du'a, you can be your truest self—broken yet hopeful, flawed yet seeking, uncertain yet trusting. Whether your words flow effortlessly or come in the form of silent tears, Allah hears them all. He does not require eloquence; He requires sincerity. And no matter how long it has been since you last turned to Him, He is always near, always ready to listen.

So speak to Him. In the quiet of the night, in the rush of your day, in the stillness of your heart. Let Du'a be your refuge, your comfort, and your reminder that you are never alone.

My Dua'a story

I remember a time when Du'a was all I had. Life felt unbearably heavy, and I carried a burden I didn't know how to put down. My heart ached with uncertainty, and my mind raced with doubts, playing out endless worst-case scenarios. No matter how much I tried to distract myself, the weight of my worries never lessened. It followed me in the quiet moments before sleep, in the emptiness of the early morning, in the spaces where I felt utterly alone.

One night, in complete exhaustion, I whispered, *Ya Allah, I don't know what to do. Please help me.*

There were no eloquent words, no structured request— just a quiet plea from a weary heart. I had no energy to formulate the "perfect" supplication or search for the most profound words. I spoke from the depths of my soul, allowing my pain to shape my Du'a. And at that moment, something shifted. I didn't feel an instant resolution, nor did my problems vanish overnight, but there was a subtle lightness, a sense that I had finally placed my burdens in the hands of the One who could carry them.

As the days passed, relief began to unfold in ways I couldn't have predicted. A friend reached out with words I needed to hear at the right time. An opportunity appeared where I thought there was none. Strength arrived when I felt I had nothing left to give. My situation didn't change immediately, but my heart did. I found the courage to take the next step, then the next, slowly realising that even in my most desperate moments, Allah had never left me.

Looking back, I realise it wasn't about saying the 'right' Du'a but about surrendering to the One who was always listening. It was about letting go of the need to control everything and trusting that even my broken, unpolished words were enough. Sometimes, Du'a is not about asking for a specific outcome—it's about placing your heart in Allah's care and knowing that whatever unfolds is part of His wisdom, mercy, and love.

Make it a daily practice

Try to weave Du'a into the fabric of your day, making it as natural as breathing. It doesn't have to be reserved for moments of desperation or hardship. Let it become the quiet rhythm that carries you through ordinary and extraordinary moments. It could be a whispered *Alhamdulillah* as you sip your morning coffee, a silent plea for strength when dealing with a difficult situation, or a heartfelt *Ya Allah, guide me* before making an important decision. Du'a is not just a practice; it is a lifeline, an ongoing conversation with the One who knows you better than you know yourself.

A Detour to Jannah

The beauty of Du'a is that it doesn't require elaborate words or perfect phrasing. Sometimes, it's a single phrase uttered in a moment of gratitude; other times, it's an unspoken yearning buried deep within your heart. Even a simple, consistent supplication—*Ya Allah, grant me ease, Ya Allah, strengthen my heart*—can renew your spirit and deepen your connection with Him. What matters is not how long or poetic your words are but how sincerely they come from within.

Don't let the fear of saying the 'wrong' Du'a hold you back. Even when your voice shakes, when words fail you, when all you can offer is a tear or a sigh—know that He understands. He hears the unspoken prayers, the longing in your silence, and the hidden cries of your soul. Du'a is not just about asking for what you need; it is an act of turning toward Him, of acknowledging that no matter what life brings, you do not walk this path alone.

And no matter how long it has been since you last made Du'a, no matter how distant you may feel, know this: Allah never tires of hearing from you. Unlike people who may grow weary or turn away, He is always near, always listening. He loves when you call upon Him, no matter how small or insignificant your request may seem.

So tonight, whenever you feel ready, lift your hands, take a deep breath, and speak to Him. Let your heart pour out its burdens, its hopes, its fears. There is no moment too late, no heart too broken, no soul too far gone

Reflecting on the Qur'an: Illuminating Your Path

The Qur'an is more than just words on a page—it is a living, breathing conversation between you and your Creator, a divine message sent to guide, heal, and illuminate your path. It is not meant to be read passively but engaged with, reflected upon, and allowed to transform your heart. Every verse carries layers of wisdom, offering comfort in distress, clarity in confusion, and direction when you feel lost.

No matter how far you have strayed, the Qur'an remains a lantern, always ready to light your way back to Allah. It does not turn away from those who have neglected it; instead, it patiently waits to be opened, its words prepared to rekindle the light of faith within you. With every recitation, every moment spent pondering its meaning; Your heart is drawn closer to the One who revealed it as a mercy to mankind.

The beauty of the Qur'an is that it speaks to you in every season of life. In moments of hardship, it reassures you that after difficulty comes ease. In times of doubt, it reminds you that Allah's knowledge and wisdom encompass all things. When you feel unworthy, it gently calls you back, reassuring you of His mercy that extends beyond what you can comprehend.

But the Qur'an is not just to be read—it is to be lived. It calls you to action, inspiring you to be kinder, more patient, and steadfast in your faith. It teaches you how to navigate life's trials, seek forgiveness, and turn every moment into an act of devotion. It is a guide, a healer, and a companion that will never leave you as long as you continue to return to it.

Approach it not as a duty but as a lifeline. Let it be your solace, your reminder, and your roadmap back to Allah. Dedicate even a small portion of your day to reading the Qur'an—whether it's a page, a few verses, or even a single ayah. What matters is not how much you read but how deeply you allow it to reach your heart.

I used to think I was failing if I couldn't read an entire page or understand Arabic perfectly. But then I learned that even one verse, reflected upon with sincerity, could change my heart. Some of the most profound moments of clarity in my life have come from reading a single verse at the right time—one that seemed to speak directly to what I was going through.

So don't rush through the verses. Let them sit with you. Some words will comfort you, others will challenge you, and some will reach parts of your heart that you didn't even know needed healing. Consider keeping a journal where you note down insights, questions, or personal reflections that arise as you read. Some days, a verse may remind you of a situation you're facing; other days, it may answer a question you hadn't even put into words. Writing it down can make your connection with the Qur'an even more personal.

The Qur'an is not just a book to be read—it is a conversation to be experienced, a light to be followed, and a refuge to return to. Open its pages with sincerity, and let it transform your heart.

Living the Qur'an

The Qur'an holds countless moments of comfort and reassurance, but one verse that deeply resonates with me is when Allah speaks to the mother of Musa (Moses) in Surah Al-Qasas. Allah commands her not to grieve, even in the midst of her profound anxiety and fear for her son:

> *"And We inspired to the mother of Musa,*
> *'Suckle him; and when you fear for him, cast*
> *him into the river, and do not fear and do not*
> *grieve. Indeed, We will return him to you and*
> *will make him one of the messengers.'"*
> *(Surah Al-Qasas 28:7)*

This verse stays with me because it speaks to the powerful reassurance Allah offers in times of unimaginable difficulty. Musa's mother was faced with a heart-wrenching decision: to send her child away, casting him into the river, trusting that Allah would protect him. It was an act of complete surrender, yet Allah, in His infinite mercy, told her not to fear or grieve. He promised her that her child would return, and not only that—he would be raised to fulfil a great purpose.

Reflect on how powerful this command is. It was not just a comfort; it was a promise. Allah's words to her remind us that no matter how bleak or uncertain our circumstances may seem, Allah's plan is always greater than our fears. His mercy surpasses our understanding, and He will never abandon us in distress.

This verse reminds me that there is always hope, even when we cannot see the way forward. No matter what we are facing, no matter how overwhelming it seems, Allah is always near, and His plan is far more perfect than anything we could ever imagine. Musa's mother was told not to grieve, and Allah fulfilled His promise, returning her son to her and making him one of the greatest messengers.

I remind myself of this verse whenever I feel overwhelmed or burdened by worry. It helps me find peace in knowing that Allah's plan is unfolding in ways I may not understand, but His mercy is constant, and His promises are true. Like the mother of Musa, we can, too, place our trust in Allah, knowing that He is always watching over us and guiding us through our darkest moments.

Small Steps, Big Transformation

Rebuilding your connection with Allah isn't about achieving perfection overnight or having all the answers at once. It's not about expecting yourself to suddenly become someone you're not or instantly feeling a profound shift in your relationship with Him. Rather, it's about understanding that this journey is gradual growth—a path that unfolds through patience, consistency, and sincerity.

Reconnecting with Allah is much like the gentle nurturing of a plant. At first, you might only see small changes, but with care and persistence, you will witness the growth of something beautiful over time. No matter how seemingly insignificant, each small action adds depth to your connection with the Divine. Whether it's a quiet moment of remembrance after a long day, a prayer with sincerity even when you're tired, or a gentle recitation of a verse from the Qur'an, these small acts of worship are the building blocks of your relationship with Allah.

One of the most powerful things to understand is that every effort counts. You may not notice immediate changes but know that each moment spent in remembrance, prayer, or reflection is an investment in your heart. These actions don't have to be grand or spectacular; they need to come from a place of sincerity and consistency.

For instance, maybe you've struggled with consistently making your five daily prayers, and that's all right. If you can make even one prayer with complete focus and devotion, it is a step in the right direction. The same goes for your du'a or supplication. It's not about having the perfect words but about opening your heart, even if only for a few moments, and turning to Allah in your own way.

As you continue along this path, you'll notice a shift—not all at once, but slowly. Your heart, once heavy or distracted, will begin to feel lighter. Your thoughts will become more focused on Allah, and the world around you will seem to change as you grow more attuned to His presence. There may still be moments of doubt or struggle, but each of those moments becomes an opportunity to turn back to Him, to ask for strength, and to trust that He is always near, guiding you through each step of your journey.

The beauty of this journey is that it's never about perfection. It's about sincere efforts, even in the face of imperfections. Every day is a new chance to build that connection, to strengthen your faith, and to draw closer to Allah. And the most incredible thing is that no matter where you are on your journey, Allah is always ready to welcome you back with open arms. His mercy is limitless, and He is ever-patient with His creation.

So, take heart in knowing that each small step you take matters. The cumulative effect of these small, intentional acts of worship gradually transforms your heart, restores your connection with Allah, and brings you closer to the peace and contentment you seek. Don't rush the process— trust that Allah's timing is perfect and that every sincere effort is seen and rewarded. Keep going, one step at a time, and know that the beauty lies in the journey itself.

Consistency Over Perfection

It's easy to believe it's not worth attempting if you can't do everything flawlessly. However, that's not how Allah regards your efforts. Every minor step is significant.

Maybe today, you can only spare an extra minute of reflection after Salah. Maybe you quietly say a heartfelt Du'a before bed. You might even find a moment to read one verse of the Qur'an. Although these acts may seem trivial, they accumulate like drops of water filling a well The Prophet peace be upon him said:

> *"The most beloved deeds to Allah are those that are consistent, even if they are small."*
> *(Bukhari Hadith 6465)*

Your sincerity matters more than your speed. Keep going, even if it's slow.

Embracing the Process

Some days, you will feel spiritually connected—your Salah will bring you peace, your Du'a will flow effortlessly, and the Qur'an will speak directly to your heart. On other days, you may struggle. Your prayers may feel rushed, your mind distracted, your heart distant.

And that's okay.

Faith is not a straight line. There will be ups and downs, moments of clarity and moments of struggle. Instead of feeling defeated on the hard days, embrace them as part of the journey. Each day is a new opportunity to return, try again, and let the light of Allah gradually fill the empty spaces.

Celebrating Progress

We often underestimate our achievements, believing they're too insignificant to matter. Yet, every act of worship, every sincere prayer, and every time you choose Allah over distractions has immense value. Though they may seem small at the time, Allah deeply cherished these moments. They represent progress on your journey and a reaffirmation of your commitment to Him.

Consider where you stood a year ago. Have you made even a tiny step forward? If yes, that's a win, no matter how small it may seem. Acknowledge your progress and express gratitude for the guidance that has led you here.

When done consistently, even the smallest actions can lead to great changes over time. The key is to recognise and appreciate these small wins, understanding that they are the foundation for bigger transformations.

Waiting for the "perfect" moment or the "right" circumstances often holds us back. The truth is, there is no perfect time to start—there's only now. You don't need to wait until you feel ready or until everything aligns perfectly.

Start where you are, with what you have. No matter how imperfect, every small step you take today is a step closer to Allah. Whether it's offering your prayers on time, reading even a few verses from the Qur'an, or simply making Du'a from your heart, these are the moments that shape your relationship with Allah.

Every small action, performed with sincerity, holds the potential to transform your heart and bring you closer to the One who has been waiting for you all along. Trust that your efforts are never in vain. The consistency, even in the smallest deeds, matters most in Allah's eyes. So, don't wait for the perfect time—begin now, and let every step bring you closer to His mercy and light.

Exercise: A Small Step Plan

Reflect: Write down three small actions you can take daily to strengthen your connection with Allah. Keep them simple and realistic (e.g., making Du'a after Fajr, reading one verse of the Qur'an daily, or praying one Salah with full concentration).

Commit: Choose one of these actions and focus on it consistently for the next seven days.

Track Your Progress: At the end of the week, reflect on how this small step improved your connection with Allah. If you feel ready, add another habit the following week.

Your Journey Back to Light

Reconnecting with Allah is a deeply personal journey that unfolds through each prayer, every Du'a, and every word of the Qur'an you cherish. It's about returning to the fundamental truths that ground your soul and recognising that transformation comes not from a single grand act but from many small steps taken with love and determination.

As you progress, remember that every effort you invest, every moment dedicated to Allah, is a powerful testament to your commitment to His light. The journey may be slow, and progress might sometimes feel subtle; however, trust that you are strengthening a more enduring connection with the Divine with each small, consistent action.

> *"Ya Allah, I come to You as I am, with all my flaws and struggles. Strengthen my heart and guide my steps back to You. Help me be consistent in my worship, sincere in my intentions, and patient in my journey. Let my small efforts be a means of drawing closer to Your mercy and love. Ya Allah, never let me stray far from You, and when I do, bring me back with even more love and conviction. Ameen.*

CHAPTER NINE
NAVIGATING THROUGH MODERN CHALLENGES

My mornings used to belong to the algorithm. Before my eyes adjusted to daylight, before my lips could murmur *"Alhamdulillah,"* my thumb would already be scrolling. The glow of the screen replaced the glow of dawn—TikTok dances at 5 AM instead of Tahajjud, Twitter rage before Fajr adhan, Instagram envy souring the sweetness of gratitude. I'd stagger out of bed, my mind a browser with 100 tabs open, my heart a corrupted file, and my soul lagging like a weak Wi-Fi signal. By the time I faced the Qiblah, my salah felt like a buffering video—stuttering, disconnected, never fully loading.

I told myself it was "normal." *Everyone's glued to their phones. It's just how the world works now.* But my spirit knew the truth: I was outsourcing my consciousness to Silicon Valley. My apps weren't tools but Trojan horses, smuggling distraction into sacred spaces.
The Prophet peace be upon him warned:

> *"A person will be brought to account on the Day of Judgment for their time"* (Tirmidhi).

Yet here I was, squandering the prime hours Allah gifted me—hours meant for reflection, worship, and intention—on viral trends and comment-section wars.

The Algorithm vs. the Adhan

My phone knew me better than I knew myself. It fed me content calibrated to my insecurities: luxury cars I couldn't afford, "perfect" Muslim influencers whose highlight reels shamed my struggles, political outrage that left me too drained to pray. My *Du'as* became transactional—quick DMs to Allah between emails. My Qur'an app gathered digital dust, buried beneath Instagram and WhatsApp. I was a user, not a worshipper—a consumer, not a servant. But Allah's mercy is the ultimate software update. One Ramadan, after snoozing Fajr for the thousandth time, I opened my screen-time report: 6.7 hours daily. Six hours— *a full third of my waking life*—lost to mindless scrolling. The data didn't lie: I'd spent more time liking posts than listening to Qur'an, more hours doomscrolling than in Sujood. My heart, that divine Wi-Fi router meant to connect me to Allah, was offline.

Ctrl+Alt+Delete: Rebooting My Relationship with Tech

I didn't quit cold turkey. I couldn't. But I began small:

1. Digital Fajr: No screens until after sunrise prayer. I charged my phone in the kitchen, not my bedroom. The first words I spoke each day became *"Allahumma bika asbahna"* (O Allah, by You we enter the morning), not *"Let me check notifications."*
2. App Accountability: Deleted TikTok. Turned

Instagram grayscale. Set a Qur'an widget on my home screen. Every time I unlocked my phone, Surah Al-Fatihah stared back, asking: *"Is this scroll worth your soul's corrosion?"*

3. Notifications Offline: Silenced non-essential alerts. Group chats could wait; Allah's remembrance couldn't.

The withdrawal was real. My thumb twitched for the dopamine drip of likes. But slowly, the silence began to heal me.

From Scrolling to Soul-Scrolling

I replaced digital rituals with divine ones:

- Surah Ad-Duha > Social Stories: Instead of posting sunrise pics, I recited *"By the morning brightness, and the night when it grows still..."* (93:1-2).
- Dhikr Downloads: I used app blockers to redirect me to Dhikr counters. *"SubhanAllah"* replaced endless scrolls.
- Digital Sadaqah: Shared Qur'an verses instead of memes. Texted friends *"JazakAllah khair"* instead of gossip.

> *The Prophet peace be upon him said, "Take advantage of five before five..."—*
> *including your free time before preoccupation (Ahmad).*

My "free time" wasn't free—it was a loan from Allah, and I'd been bankrupting myself.

Relapses happened. I'd still binge Netflix some nights, or sneak a scroll during work breaks. But Allah's mercy is the ultimate cloud storage—every *Astaghfirullah* restored deleted blessings. I learned to pray even when distracted, repent even when ashamed, and trust that Allah's algorithm of mercy outranks Silicon Valley's.

Today, my mornings belong to Allah. My phone stays dark until I've prayed Fajr and thanked Him for another day to *live*, not just exist. The apps that once drained me now serve my Deen: Quran apps with verse reminders, prayer times synced to my calendar, podcasts about sabr instead of celebrity drama.

The Prophet peace be upon him said, *"The best of you are those who learn the Qur'an and teach it"* (Bukhari). I'm no scholar, but I teach now too—by sharing screen-time hacks for spiritual growth, by modelling that Muslims can master tech without being mastered by it.
If my story resonates, know this:

- **You're not "weak"**—you're battling billion-dollar apps engineered to addict you.
- **Start small**: Silence one app. Pray one salah offline. Let Allah's mercy patch your connection.
- **Allah > Algorithm**: His "content" never expires—the Qur'an, the stars, the breath in your lungs.

A Detour to Jannah

Allah says:

> *"And remember your Lord within yourself,*
> *humbly and with fear, without loudness, in*
> *the mornings and evenings. And do not be*
> *among the heedless" (7:205).*

The digital Dunya will keep buzzing. But you—you can choose to mute the noise and tune into the Eternal Signal.

Practical Tips to Take Control

Set Boundaries: Decide when and how you'll use social media. Give yourself designated "no phone" times—especially in the morning and before bed. Instead of waking up and immediately scrolling, start your day with *Bismillah*, a few moments of gratitude, or reciting a verse of the Quran. Before bed, replace screen time with a moment of quiet reflection or Du'a.

Follow with Purpose: Who you follow shapes what you see, and what you see influences your heart. Unfollow accounts that bring negativity, comparison, or temptation into your life. Instead, fill your feed with reminders of faith, uplifting messages, and beneficial knowledge. Let your timeline be a place of inspiration rather than distraction.

Replace the scroll: If you find yourself reaching for your phone out of habit, pause. What if you opened the Quran app and read just one verse instead of mindlessly scrolling? What if you made a quick Du'a? What if you stepped outside, took a deep breath, and reconnected with the present moment? These tiny shifts, done consistently, can transform your relationship with social media.

Peer Pressure: Staying Firm When You Feel Alone

At a time in my life, I was surrounded by people who didn't take my faith seriously. They would say things like, *"Why are you always so strict?"* or *"Come on, just loosen up a little— it's not that deep."*

At first, I laughed it off, telling myself their words didn't affect me. But slowly, I found myself hesitating before mentioning Allah in conversations. I started feeling awkward about excusing myself to pray. I would stay silent when someone made a joke that crossed a line, even though I knew I should have spoken up.

That's when I realised something powerful: the company we keep shapes the person we become.

The Prophet peace be upon him said:

> *"A person is upon the religion of his close friend, so let one of you look at whom he befriends." (Abu Dawood Hadith 4833; Tirmidhi Hadith 2378)*

We like to think that we are immune to influence and can spend time with people whose values contradict ours and remain unchanged. But the truth is, influence is subtle. It's in the way we start downplaying our beliefs to fit in, the way we become desensitised to haram and the way we begin seeking approval from people rather than from Allah.

So, how do we stay strong when we feel alone?

Find Your People

Even one righteous friend can make all the difference. Surround yourself with people who uplift your faith, remind you to pray, and bring out the best in you. And if you haven't found them yet, be that person for someone else. When you prioritise faith in your friendships, you attract those who do the same.

Be Confident in Your Identity

When someone questions your choices, respond with kindness but stand firm. You don't need to argue or prove yourself—be unwavering in your devotion to Allah. Your faith is not a weakness, and your relationship with Allah is not up for debate. Hold your head high, knowing that your strength comes from Him.

Set Boundaries with Love

Not every friend will align with your values, and that's okay. But if someone repeatedly pushes you toward things that pull you away from Allah, it's worth reassessing their role in your life. You can love people from a distance while protecting your heart and Iman.

Make Du'a for Righteous Company

One of the most powerful things you can do is ask

Allah to bless you with companions who bring you closer to Him. I experienced the impact of this Du'a— how Allah removed certain people from my life and replaced them with better company when I least expected it. Trust me, He listens.

> *"O Allah, grant me righteous companionship that helps me obey You and brings me closer to You." Amen.*

Remember that Allah is always with you if you ever feel like you're walking this path alone. And He will place the right people in your life at the right time. Stay patient, stay firm, and trust His plan.

Finding Halal Entertainment Without Feeling Left Out

Let's be honest—it's hard to escape the hyper-sexualized and materialistic nature of entertainment today. From music to movies and shows, it can often feel like every form of media promotes values that directly conflict with what we believe. In a world where social media influencers and mainstream media seem to celebrate things that go against our faith, it's easy to feel isolated or like you're missing out.

I've been there—standing in a circle of friends, everyone talking about the latest show or song, and I'd feel this wave of guilt wash over me. *"Should I be watching that too? Am I being too strict?"* There was a time when I would watch those shows, even though I knew they didn't align with my values, to avoid feeling left out. But deep down, I knew I was compromising my peace, and that didn't sit right with me.

Over time, I realised something important: Being true to your values doesn't mean living a boring or isolated life. You can have as much fun as possible while staying aligned with your faith. It's all about shifting your perspective and being intentional about your choices.

Here are some alternative ideas for entertainment that align with our faith.

Books & Podcasts

There's a whole world of knowledge out there waiting to inspire you— without the guilt! Instead of binge-watching shows that leave you empty, dive into books or podcasts that nurture your soul. I found some incredible authors who write about self-improvement, Islamic history, and even fiction that promotes positive values. Podcasts are another great way to engage with topics that interest you—spirituality, mental health, or personal growth.
These resources allow you to learn while relaxing, nourishing your heart and mind.

Outdoor Adventures

Spending time outdoors is one of the most fulfilling and refreshing ways to connect with Allah's creation. Whether it's a picnic in the park, hiking in the mountains, or even just walking by the water, nature has this incredible way of grounding you and reminding you of the beauty of the world Allah created. I love to take my kids out for a walk, exploring nature together—it's a peaceful way to unwind, reflect, and make dua as we breathe in the fresh air.

Halal Gatherings

Who says you must stay inside watching endless episodes of something to have fun? Try hosting or joining halal gatherings with family or friends.

Game nights, cooking together, or having deep, meaningful conversations can be just as fulfilling, if not more, than any entertainment you might find on a screen. A few months ago, I hosted a cook-and-eat session with some close friends. We shared recipes, laughed, and made delicious food together. It was a fulfilling experience, and I did not feel like I was "missing out."

I used to feel guilty for watching shows that didn't align with my values, but I didn't know how to stop. I told myself, *"It's just entertainment; it won't hurt."* But after a while, I realised that it weighed down my heart.

That's when I decided to make small changes, switching to educational content, nature documentaries, and light-hearted halal entertainment.

Switching from mindless shows to shows aligned with my values wasn't as hard as I thought. Slowly, I replaced my TV time with something more productive, like reading or listening to podcasts on Islamic teachings, self-development, and motivation. Little by little, I noticed a difference in how I felt—my heart felt lighter, my mind clearer, and I didn't feel like I was "missing out" anymore.

> You don't have to live unfulfilled to stay true to your faith. With some intention, you can enjoy entertainment that aligns with your values while still feeling connected to the world.

May Allah guide you to the entertainment that nourishes your soul, uplifts your spirit, and helps you grow closer to Him.

Final Thoughts: Walking the Middle Path

Islam doesn't ask us to cut ourselves off from the world; it teaches us how to engage with it in a way that protects our hearts and strengthens our faith. You don't have to be perfect—you must be aware, intentional, and willing to correct courses when needed.

Reflection Exercise:

Take a few moments to reflect on your habits and influences. Write down:

1. One social media habit you want to change.
2. One way you can strengthen your faith circle.
3. One form of entertainment you can replace with something more beneficial.

"Ya Allah, keep my heart firm on Your path.

> *Help me navigate the challenges of this*
> *world without losing sight of my purpose.*
> *Replace what harms me with what brings me*
> *closer to You. Make halal fulfilling for me*
> *and haram distasteful to my heart. Ameen."*

My dear sister or brother, this journey isn't about being perfect—it's about being aware, making small changes, and continuously turning back to Allah. And the beautiful thing? With every step you take toward Him, He takes multiple steps toward you. Keep walking. Keep striving. And trust that you are never alone in this.

PART FOUR:
TRANSFORMING THE
DETOUR INTO A BLESSING

CHAPTER TEN
LESSONS FROM THE
SCENIC ROUTE

Imagine a traveller who strays from the path, unknowingly taking a turn that wasn't part of their plan. At first, they don't even realise they've gone off course. The road beneath their feet feels the same, the trees still stand tall, and the sun filters through the canopy above. But as they press forward, something changes. The path becomes uneven, the once-familiar landscape now foreign. Landmarks they once relied on have disappeared. Anxiety creeps in—where did they go wrong? Why didn't they notice the signs earlier? Frustration builds with every uncertain step. They retrace their journey in their mind, searching for the exact moment they veered off course.

But something unexpected happens as they walk on, expecting only more difficulty. Instead of a dead end, they stumble upon a breathtaking valley untouched by time. The golden wildflowers sway gently in the breeze, their fragrance filling the air. A crystal-clear stream winds through the land, its water so pure that it shimmers in the sunlight. Birds sing from the trees, their melodies harmonising with the rustling leaves. It's a place of peace, beauty, and renewal—a place they never would have found had they not gotten lost.

A Detour to Jannah

Your detour is that valley.

What if the moments in your life that felt like wrong turns were actually guiding you to something greater? What if the struggles, missteps, and confusion all led you to a place of growth, clarity, and a deeper connection with Allah?

There was once a young man who had grown up surrounded by faith. He knew the words of the Qur'an, had memorised du'as, and had been taught the beauty of worship. His childhood was filled with the sound of adhan, the warmth of Ramadan nights, and the comfort of knowing he belonged to something greater than himself. But somewhere along the way, life pulled him in another direction. The world's distractions whispered louder than the call to prayer. Salah became occasional, the Qur'an sat unopened, and the presence of Allah in his heart faded into the background noise of daily life.

At first, he hardly noticed the shift. But as time passed, an unease settled within him, like a weight pressing down on his soul. Guilt lurked beneath the surface, yet he buried it beneath excuses: *I'm too far gone. Maybe one day I'll change. Maybe later. Maybe when I have more time, but* "later" never came.

Then, one evening, a short video appeared as he scrolled mindlessly through his phone. Just a simple reminder about Allah's mercy—nothing extraordinary. But one line struck him like lightning: *"Allah loves to forgive, so why do you believe He won't forgive you?"*

Something within him cracked. For the first time in years, his heart stirred. It wasn't a grand revelation or a dramatic moment—it was a whisper, a tug, a nudge toward something he had been avoiding for too long. That night, he made wudu and stood for prayer. Not because he felt pure, but because he finally understood that purity comes from turning back, not from never falling.

His journey back to Allah wasn't instant. It wasn't a single prayer that changed everything. It was slow, unsteady, filled with moments of struggle. There were days when he felt the weight of his past pressing down on him, whispering that he wasn't worthy of redemption. But each time he prayed, opened the Qur'an, and whispered a du'a, he found himself taking another step forward.

Years later, he runs an Islamic reminder page on social media, sharing messages of hope and mercy with others. He knows that somewhere out there, someone might be scrolling through their phone, needing to hear what he once needed.

No matter how far you've strayed, His mercy is always within reach. The beauty of Allah's forgiveness is that it does not require you to erase your past—only to turn back with sincerity. What feels like a detour may be the very road that guides you home.

This chapter invites you to revisit your detour—not as a

mistake but as a divine syllabus. Every stumble, tear, and moment you whispered, *"Why me?"* was a lesson curated by Allah to sculpt your soul into something stronger, softer, and more radiant than you could have imagined.

The Qur'an assures us:

> *"And We will surely test you with something of fear and hunger and loss... But give good tidings to the patient—those who, when disaster strikes them, say, 'Indeed we belong to Allah, and indeed to Him we will return.'"*
> *(Surah Al-Baqarah 2:155-156)*

Your scenic route was never a punishment. It was a classroom.

So let me ask you:

- *What wildflowers have bloomed in your valley of struggle?*

- *What hymns of mercy has Allah sung over you in the silence?*

- *What lessons has your detour gifted you that you never would have learned on a straight path?*

What Your Detour Reveals About You

Sometimes, the moments we feel furthest from Allah are not signs of abandonment but invitations to reflect, grow, and rediscover His presence in our lives. Every struggle, misstep, and detour you've taken carries a lesson— whether in resilience, humility, or the boundless nature of Allah's mercy.

A Detour to Jannah

These experiences are not meant to define you by your past but to shape your journey forward with deeper understanding and renewed faith.

Because in the end, no matter how far you've wandered or how lost you've felt, there is always a way back. And when you take that first step, you'll realise He was never far away.

This exercise is designed to guide you through that reflection, helping you uncover the hidden wisdom within your experiences. Looking back with honesty and sincerity, you may see how even your lowest moments held glimpses of Allah's guidance, nudging you toward Him in ways you never expected.

Take your time with it. Find a quiet space, grab a journal, and allow yourself to write freely. Be honest about your struggles, but also gentle with yourself—because every step, even the ones that felt like stumbles, has brought you to this moment of self-discovery.

Step 1: Identify 3 Challenges from Your Detour

Think about a period in your life when you felt disconnected from Allah. What were the biggest struggles you faced? Write down three of them. These could be:

- *Falling into harmful habits*

- *Doubting your faith*

A Detour to Jannah

- O *Feeling isolated from the Muslim community*

- O *Struggling with prayer*

- O *Being in an unhealthy relationship*

- O *Dealing with guilt and shame*

Step 2: Ask Yourself 3 Questions About Each Challenge

For every challenge, reflect on the following:

How did this struggle reveal my strengths? Even in your lowest moments, you displayed resilience in ways you may not have noticed. Maybe you held on to hope, even when it was dim. Perhaps you kept searching for answers, even when doubt clouded your mind. Recognising your strengths helps you see that you *never truly gave up.*

What weaknesses did it expose? This is not about self-blame—it is about self-awareness. What habits or thought patterns contributed to your struggle? Did you rely too much on your emotions instead of Allah's promises? Did you seek validation from the wrong places? Identifying these patterns helps you move forward with clarity.

How did Allah show up in this moment? No matter how far we drift, Allah never abandons us. Think about the ways He guided you back, even in small ways. Did He place someone in your life to remind you of Him? Did He give you

156

a sudden moment of clarity? Did He soften your heart at just the right time? Recognising Allah's presence in your past struggles strengthens your trust in Him for the future.

Example Reflection

Challange

"I stopped praying during a depressive episode."

Strength:

"Even though I was not praying, I kept making du'a, begging Allah for help—even when I felt nothing."

Weakness:

"I based my worship on how I felt instead of Allah's worthiness. I realised I needed to pray because I needed Him, not just when I felt connected."

How Allah Showed Up:

"He sent a friend who texted me every morning saying, 'Let us pray Fajr together.' That one message pulled me back into the rhythm of prayer."

Your struggles are not signs of failure—they are part of the journey. Every hardship, detour, and lesson shapes you into a stronger believer. Looking back, you will see that even in the moments you felt furthest from Allah, He was never far from you.

The Hidden Curriculum

He is Al-Wali (The Protector) in Disguise

A Detour to Jannah

Your detour might have felt like abandonment, but look closer:

- *Lost friendships?* He shielded you from toxic influences.
- *Financial strain?* He taught you reliance on Him over wealth.
- *Failure?* He rerouted you to a better path.

He Is Al-Latif (The Subtle) in the Details

Notice the "small" mercies woven into your struggle:

- A Quran verse that resonated deeply.
- A stranger's kindness at your lowest moment.
- A sudden moment of clarity during dua.

Exercise: The Mercy Timeline

1. Draw a timeline of your detour.
2. Mark moments where Allah's subtle guidance appeared.
3. Write: *"Allah was teaching me _____ here."*

How Detours Forge Unshakable Iman

Trials Reveal Your True Capacity

The Quran says:

> *"Allah does not burden a soul*

*beyond what   it can bear." (Surah
Baqarah 2:286)*

Your detour was not a random act of cruelty—it was a
divine stress test, revealing reservoirs of strength you
never knew existed. Think of it like this: A diamond is just
coal under pressure. A seed must crack open to grow.
You? You have been weathering storms, and somewhere in
the chaos, your roots dug deeper, your heart grew fiercer,
and your faith became unbreakable.

Story of the Unseen Fortress:

Zara had always told herself that she was fine as long as
she believed in Allah. *"I know what's right,"* she would say,
even as she ignored the guilt in her heart. At first, it was just
small compromises—music that dulled her remembrance,
conversations that blurred boundaries, late nights spent in
places she knew she didn't belong. But sin is like
quicksand—the deeper you go, the harder it is to pull
yourself out.

One night, she came home feeling hollow after a gathering
she knew she shouldn't have attended. None of the
temporary highs, the fleeting moments of excitement, filled
the emptiness inside. As she scrolled through her phone, her
eyes landed on a reminder someone had shared:

*"Do not be like those who forgot Allah, so He
made them forget themselves." (Qur'an
59:19)*

Her heart clenched. **Had she forgotten herself?** Had she let her soul starve while chasing the illusions of this world? Tears welled in her eyes as she placed her phone down and whispered, *"Ya Allah, I don't want to be lost anymore."*

That night, for the first time in months, she prayed. It was awkward, shaky, and filled with shame—but it was real. And it was the first step back. *"I used to think I had to be perfect to return to Allah,"* she says. *"But I realised He never asked for perfection—only sincerity."*

Reflect:

What storms have you weathered? How did they prove Allah's trust in your resilience?

Struggles Deepen Empathy

Pain is a universal language, spoken in tear-streaked faces, quiet sighs, and the weight of unspoken sorrow. When you have tasted despair and wrestled with the shadows of your own struggles, you gain an intimate understanding of suffering—one that transcends mere words. You begin to recognise its presence in the eyes of a stranger, in the hesitance of a friend who says, *"I am fine"*, but doesn't quite meet your gaze. You hear it in the cracks of a trembling voice, in the silence that lingers too long.

Your detour—the hardships, mistakes, and moments you thought would break you—has gifted you something rare: a lens that sees past the masks people wear. It allows you to notice the silent wars raging within every heart, to extend a hand where others might walk past, and to offer comfort that comes not from pity but from knowing.

And that is a gift because those who have walked through darkness can best guide others toward the light.

Story of the Wounded Healer

Hassan had spent years chasing wealth, convinced that success would bring him peace. Deals were made, corners were cut, and prayers became an afterthought. The more he gained, the emptier he felt. Then, one night, a sudden phone call shattered his world—his younger brother had passed away unexpectedly.

"I stood at his grave, my hands full of dirt, my heart full of regret," Hassan recalls. *"He always reminded me to pray, to give, to prepare for the next life. And I always said, 'Later.'"*

But later, he never came for his brother. That night, Hassan fell to his knees in sujood for the first time in years—not out of routine, but out of desperation and longing.

Slowly, he rebuilt what he had neglected—his connection with Allah, his family, his purpose. He started using his wealth to fund orphanages, build wells, and support struggling families. *"The money I once worshipped is now my tool for good,"* he says. *"I lost my brother, but through him, I found my way back to Allah."*

Reflect:

How has your pain equipped you to serve others? Who needs your unique form of empathy today?

Detours Shatter Illusions of Control

We cling to plans like lifelines—"If I work harder, pray more, follow the rules, life will bend to my will." We map out our futures precisely, believing that certainty is our right. But then, the detour hits. Jobs vanish. Relationships fracture. Health fails. The path we built so carefully crumbles beneath our feet, leaving us in the wreckage of expectations we once thought unshakable.

At first, there is only confusion. "Why, Allah? I did everything right." Frustration follows, then fear—what if our plans cannot hold us? But in that space of uncertainty, something profound happens. When the noise of our own will fades, we finally hear the whisper that was always there:

"I am Al-Hakim (The All-Wise). Let Me lead."

It is in surrender, not control, that we find peace. In losing our plans, we make space for something greater—His plan. The hardship that felt like a punishment was a course correction. The door that slammed shut wasn't rejection but redirection. And the delay we resented was mercy in disguise.

Sometimes, we must be stripped of everything we thought we needed to realise that Allah is all we ever truly did.

Story of the Perfect Plan That Was Not:

Kareem had it all mapped out: graduate at the top of his class, land a six- figure job and marry by 25. However, when chronic illness derailed his career, he spiralled into anger. *"I had done everything 'right'—why was Allah punishing me?"* he raged. Years later, as a counsellor for chronically ill youth, he realised: *"My 'perfect' plan would have made me arrogant and empty. Allah's detour made me humble and whole."*

Reflect:

What illusion of control did your detour shatter? How did surrendering to Allah's plan bring unexpected peace?

The Art of Sacred Reflection: Turning Lessons Into Legacy

Daily Gratitude for the Journey

Each night, ask:

- O *"What did this day teach me about myself?"*
- O *"How did Allah soften my heart through today's struggles?"*

Pay It Forward

Use your story to guide others. The Prophet peace be upon him said :

> *"Whoever relieves a believer of a hardship in this world, Allah will relieve them of a hardship on the Day of Judgment." (Muslim Hadith 2699)*

Your Detour Was Never a Mistake

Allah says:

> *"It may be that you hate a thing while it is good for you, and it may be that you love a thing while it is bad for you. Allah knows, and you do not know." (Surah Al-Baqarah 2:216)*

Your detour was not a setback—it was a lesson. Every challenge, tear, and doubt you faced was an opportunity to grow, understand, and draw closer to the One who knows what's best for you.

The Detour Diploma

1. Write a certificate "awarding" yourself for lessons learned:

- *"Graduate of Resilience."*
- *"Master of Trust in Al-Qadir (The All-Powerful)."*

2. Display it where you will see it daily—a reminder that your struggles were never in vain.

CHAPTER ELEVEN
THE POWER OF GRATITUDE AND DHIKR

I used to think gratitude was something you felt when things were going well—when life was easy, duas were answered the way you wanted, and blessings were obvious. It was easy to say Alhamdulillah when I had a good day, my children were happy, and I felt strong and capable.

However, then life took its unexpected turn.

My illness changed everything. Suddenly, things I had taken for granted—like waking up feeling rested, walking without pain, or having the energy to play with my children—became struggles. I felt trapped in a body that was not cooperating, and my heart became heavy with frustration.

At first, I resisted. I fought against my reality, clinging to how things used to be. I prayed for healing, normalcy, and my old strength to return. But, when it did not, the frustration deepened. I found myself asking, *why me? Why now?*

I remember lying in bed after another exhausting day one night, feeling utterly drained. The weight of my struggles pressed down on me, and I could not muster enough energy to make a long *dua*. My body was aching, my heart was restless, and my mind was drowning in worries. All I could do was whisper, *Ya Allah, help me.*

At that moment, a thought settled in my heart, almost like a whisper in my soul:

What if I stopped focusing on what was missing and started noticing what was still there?

What if, instead of resenting the pain, I thanked Allah for the moments of relief? What if I saw them as reminders to turn to Him instead of feeling frustrated by my limits?

What if I embraced gratitude in the middle of the storm instead of waiting for things to be perfect?

I had spent so long thinking that gratitude was reserved for the good days, that *Alhamdulillah* was only for the moments that made me smile. However, *Alhamdulillah* is not just for ease—it is for every moment, even the ones that bring us to our knees.

That night, I committed to starting my days with Alhamdulillah, no matter what, not just when things were easy or when I felt strong but especially when I didn't.

That tiny shift changed everything.

At first, it felt unnatural. How could I say *Alhamdulillah* when my body was aching? Unlike my old self, how could I be grateful when I felt so weak?

But as I made an effort to focus on gratitude, I started noticing things I had overlooked before: the way my children still ran to hug me, even on my worst days; the warmth of my home; the ability to breathe still, think, and feel; the way Allah, in His mercy, still gave me moments of joy in between the hardship.

I realised that even in my pain, there were blessings. Even in my exhaustion, there were reasons to say *Alhamdulillah*. And I began to understand a powerful truth:

Gratitude is not about waiting for perfect conditions. It is about seeing Allah's mercy even in the imperfection.

Allah tells us in the Qur'an:

> *"If you are grateful, I will surely increase you*
> *[in favour]; but if you deny, indeed, My*
> *punishment is severe." (Surah Ibrahim 14:7)*

I used to think this meant that if I said *Alhamdulillah*, Allah would give me more of what I wanted. But now, I understand it differently. Gratitude shifts your heart. It increases your awareness of blessings that were already there. It does not necessarily change your situation but changes how you see it.

And that is a gift greater than anything the Dunya can offer.

The Prophet peace be upon him taught us that gratitude is not just a feeling—it is a way of life. He said:

A Detour to Jannah

> *"Amazing is the affair of the believer! Verily, all of his affairs are good, and this is not for anyone except the believer. If something good happens to him, he is grateful, and that is good for him. If something bad happens to him, he is patient, and that is good for him."*
> *(Sahih Muslim 2999)*

This hadith used to sound beautiful in theory, but I struggled to apply it. How could difficulty be good for me? How could pain be something to be grateful for?

But slowly, I started to understand. My struggles had pushed me closer to Allah in a way that ease never did. My illness forced me to slow down, to reflect, to turn to Him in a way I had never done before. It softened my heart, stripped away my illusions of control, and made me realise how much I needed Him.

And was that not a blessing in itself?

Alhamdulillah, for the things that bring me closer to Allah, even when they hurt.

Alhamdulillah for the reminders that this life is temporary, and that Jannah is the real goal.

Alhamdulillah, for the pain that humbles me, keeps me from arrogance and teaches me patience and trust.

Alhamdulillah is not just a phrase; it is a mindset, a way of seeing the world, and a constant reminder that no matter what happens, Allah is always giving, guiding, and blessing.

The Key to a Content Heart

Allah's wisdom in the Qur'an and the teachings of the Prophet Muhammad peace be upon him offer profound insights into gratitude (shukr) as a transformative spiritual practice. Expanding on this timeless truth, we uncover layers of meaning and practical guidance to nurture a heart anchored in contentment.

Allah repeatedly emphasises gratitude as both a recognition of His endless favors and a catalyst for receiving more:

> *"If you are grateful, I will surely increase you [in favour]; but if you deny, indeed, My punishment is severe." (Surah Ibrahim 14:7)*

Another verse reminds us:

> *"If you tried to count Allah's blessings, you could never enumerate them. Indeed, humanity is [prone to] wrongdoing, ingratitude" (Qur'an 16:18).*

Gratitude is not merely an emotion—it is an act of worship, a conscious choice to acknowledge that every breath, trial, and joy is a divine gift. Even hardships carry hidden mercies, as Allah says:

> *"Perhaps you hate something while it is good for you" (Qur'an 2:216).*

Gratitude is not just about feeling happy when life is good. It is about acknowledging that every moment—good or bad—is part of Allah's divine plan for you.

Sometimes, we get caught up in waiting for the "big" things before we allow ourselves to be grateful. We wait for a promotion, healing, marriage, or ease, thinking we will feel content. But the truth is, if we do not learn to see the blessings in the present moment, we will always be chasing the next thing, never truly satisfied.

The Prophet peace be upon him taught us a beautiful perspective on gratitude:

> *"Look at those who are lower than you (in wealth and worldly matters) and do not look at those who are above you, lest you belittle the blessings of Allah (upon you)."*
>
> *(Sahih Muslim 2963)*

When I started focusing on what I *had* rather than what I lacked, I noticed blessings I had overlooked:

- The ability to still hold my children and hear their laughter.
- The fact that, despite my illness, I could still stand in prayer, even if for a short time.
- The warmth of a home, the food on my table, the air in my lungs.

Gratitude is not about ignoring pain. It is about seeing the

A Detour to Jannah

mercy of Allah even within the struggle.

The Three Dimensions of Shukr

Scholars describe gratitude as:

- **Heart:** Recognizing blessings as from Allah.

- **Tongue:** Praising Allah verbally.

- **Limbs:** Using blessings in obedience to Him. For instance, the gift of health is honoured by praying, the gift of wealth by giving charity, and the gift of time by seeking knowledge.

Gratitude is a muscle that strengthens with practice. It transforms ordinary moments into worship and trials into lessons. As Ibn Qayyim wrote, "The heart's health lies in gratitude; its illness is denial." Let us close with the Prophet's peace be upon him supplication:

"O Allah, help me remember You, express gratitude to You, and worship You in the best manner" (Sunan Abi Dawud 1522).

May our hearts find serenity in gratitude, and may Allah make us among those who *"proclaim the favors of their Lord" (Qur'an 92:19).*

Dhikr: Tethering the Heart to Allah

Life is loud. Our minds are constantly flooded with distractions— notifications, responsibilities, worries about the future. It is easy to go through an entire day without meaningfully remembering Allah.

But the beauty of *dhikr* (remembrance of Allah) is that it is a direct lifeline to Him. It is how we anchor ourselves amidst the chaos, soften our hearts, and protect ourselves from despair.

Allah says in the Qur'an:

> *"Verily, in the remembrance of Allah do hearts find rest." (Surah Ar-Ra'd 13:28)*

And the Prophet peace be upon him told us:

> *"The example of the one who remembers his Lord and the one who does not remember Him is like that of the living and the dead."*
>
> *(Sahih al-Bukhari 6407)*

Dhikr is life for the heart. And the best part? It is simple. You do not need a perfect environment. You do not need hours of free time. You can wash dishes and say SubhanAllah, Alhamdulillah, and *Allahu Akbar*. You can be driving and sending *Salawat* upon the Prophet, peace be upon him. You can lie in bed, unable to move from exhaustion, and still whisper *La ilaha illa Allah*.

I found that when I incorporated dhikr into my day—not as a separate task but as something woven into my routine—I felt lighter, more connected, and less burdened by the things I could not control.

A Practical Way to Start

If you are struggling to bring more gratitude and dhikr into your life, start small:

Morning Gratitude Habit: Before you reach for your phone in the morning, say *Alhamdulillah* for three things—no matter how small.

Daily Dhikr Moments: Choose a regular activity (like cooking, walking, or waiting at a red light) to say simple dhikr:

- *SubhanAllah wa bihamdihi, subhanAllahil azeem* (**Light on the tongue, but heavy on the scale!** – Sahih Muslim 2694)
- *Astaghfirullah* (**For constant renewal of the heart**)
- *La ilaha illa Allah* (**A reminder of our ultimate purpose**)

End the Day with Reflection: Before sleeping, think of one moment in your day that reminded you of Allah's mercy.

The Greatest Gift

One of the most powerful lessons I've learned on my journey is that gratitude and dhikr are more than just acts of worship—they are healing. They are medicine for the heart and balm for the soul. These practices do something profound: they shift your perspective, soothe your heart, and remind you that no matter what happens in this world, you are never, ever alone.

Before my illness, I did not fully appreciate the weight of

these simple acts. I took them for granted—just another part of my routine. But now, I see them as a lifeline. They keep me tethered to Allah, grounding me in moments when everything else feels chaotic or out of my control. The simple words *Alhamdulillah* and *Astaghfirullah* have become my anchor. They are the rope that pulls me back from the depths of my struggles, no matter how overwhelming they may be.

It is easy to feel distant from Allah during tough times. We feel abandoned or lose our way when the world becomes too heavy. But the beautiful thing about our relationship with Allah is that He is always there. Even when we forget Him, He never forgets us. His mercy surrounds us, even in our darkest moments. And that, my dear reader, is the greatest gift we could ever receive.

We often think we must go through something life-changing to be humbled, return to Allah, and become closer to Him. We think illness, loss, and heartbreak must come first for us to turn our hearts back to Allah. But this is not true. You do not need to wait for a life-altering moment.

You do not need to wait for hardship to strike before valuing your health, blessings, or relationship with Allah. The time to start is *now*. While you are healthy and have everything, it is the perfect time to nourish your heart with gratitude and remembrance.

The Prophet peace be upon him said:

A Detour to Jannah

> *"Take advantage of five before five: your*
> *youth before your old age, your health before*
> *your sickness, your wealth before your*
> *poverty, your free time before your busy time,*
> *and your life before your death." (Hadith,*
> *Sahih al-Jami)*

This hadith reminds us to use our gifts today—our health, time, and energy— to turn to Allah. Do not wait for a crisis to bring you to your knees. Start now, in your moments of ease, and keep nurturing your relationship with Him.

It is easy to take things for granted when life is going well. But the truth is that we have the greatest opportunity to grow closer to Allah during these times. We do not need to be humbled by hardship; we can choose to humble ourselves before Allah in our blessings, comfort, and health.

And I promise you that when you make dhikr and gratitude a consistent part of your life—when you say *Alhamdulillah* in ease and *Astaghfirullah* when you fall short—it will transform your heart. You will begin to see the beauty in every moment, even in the mundane. You will begin to recognise the blessings that have always surrounded you, even when you were too distracted to notice them.

In moments of hardship, you will feel the power of dhikr lifting you up, and you will know, deep down, that you are never alone. You are always held in Allah's mercy.

So, keep remembering, praising, and saying *Alhamdulillah*

in every moment—whether in ease or hardship. Every time you turn to Allah in gratitude and say *Astaghfirullah*, you are taking a step closer to Him.

And isn't that what our hearts are searching for? To feel His presence? To know that He is there, always guiding, always forgiving, always loving? That is the ultimate purpose of this life: to return to Allah, to find peace in His remembrance, and to know that His mercy is limitless.

You do not have to wait for hardship to remind you of this truth. Start now. In your health, in your peace, in your blessings. Make gratitude and dhikr your foundation, and you will find that Allah, in His infinite mercy, will draw you closer to Him, no matter where you are.

CHAPTER TWELVE
SURROUND YOURSELF
WITH THE RIGHT COMPANY

One of the most profound lessons I have learned on this journey is that the company you keep directly impacts your heart's state and connection with Allah. It's not just a saying—it's a truth that I've experienced deeply. In times of struggle, moments of joy, and the routine of everyday life, the people around you shape how you think, feel, and, ultimately, worship.

I used to think that my relationship with Allah was something very personal, that it depended solely on my efforts and my relationship with Him. But over time, I realised how much the people around me influenced my journey. The ones I surrounded myself with either lifted me up or pulled me down. It was not just about their advice or words but the energy they brought into my life, the example they set, and how they encouraged or discouraged me from remaining steadfast.

When surrounded by people who reminded me of Allah, encouraged me to pray and made me feel good about striving in my faith, I felt more connected to Him. Their presence was like a light source, pushing me toward goodness, reminding me of my purpose, and lifting my spirits when I was low.

A Detour to Jannah

On the other hand, when I spent time with people more concerned with worldly matters, those conversations often drained my energy and distracted me from the important things. I started to see that the company I kept profoundly impacted my mindset and actions. It shaped my thoughts, influenced the choices I made, and, unknowingly, even affected the way I viewed my relationship with Allah.

It's not always apparent at first, but it is true: the people around you will help you grow closer to Allah or steer you away from Him. If you are constantly surrounded by negativity, gossip, or people who do not value the importance of faith, it becomes harder to maintain your connection with Allah. But when you have a circle of people who remind you of Him, push you to do better, and share the same values, it becomes much easier to stay grounded in your faith.

Allah warns us about the consequences of unwise alliances:

"And keep yourself patient with those who call upon their Lord morning and evening, seeking His face. And let not your eyes pass beyond them, desiring adornments of the worldly life..." (Qur'an 18:28).

Conversely, He illustrates the regret of those who chose misguided friends:

"Oh, woe to me! I wish I had not taken so-

> *and-so as a friend! He led me away from the*
> *remembrance [of Allah] after it had come to*
> *me..." (Qur'an 25:27–29).*

These verses highlight companionship as a divine trust. Righteous friends anchor us in *dhikr* (remembrance of Allah), while toxic relationships distract us from our ultimate purpose.

The Prophet peace be upon him likened good and bad company to two powerful metaphors:

> *"The example of a good companion and a*
> *bad companion is like that of a perfume seller*
> *and a blacksmith. The perfume seller may*
> *give you some fragrance, or you may buy*
> *from him, or at least enjoy his pleasant scent.*
> *As for the blacksmith, he may burn your*
> *clothes, or you may endure his repulsive*
> *fumes" (Sahih al-Bukhari 2101, Sahih*
> *Muslim 2628).*

This analogy underscores how companionship subtly influences our thoughts, habits, and spiritual "scent." The hadith about faith being tied to friendship ("A person is upon the religion of their friend") further reminds us that our social circles are not neutral—they shape our identity and priorities

The Prophet Muhammad peace be upon him said:

> *A person is likely to follow the faith of his*

> *friend, so look to whom you befriend." (Abu Dawood Hadith 4833)*

This hadith made me realise that the friendships I nurtured weren't just about companionship; they were about my spiritual health. I came to understand that if I wanted to be close to Allah, I needed to surround myself with people who reflected His light, who reminded me of my purpose, and who would encourage me on the path of righteousness.

It wasn't just about finding people who shared my struggles or frustrations but also those who would help me grow spiritually, even when difficult. The right company can pull you out of a dark place, reminding you to turn back to Allah, seek His mercy, and always strive for more, no matter how many times you fall.

So, I encourage you to reflect on the relationships you have. Ask yourself:

Do the people around me inspire me to be better in my faith?

Do they remind me of Allah, His mercy, and the beauty of this journey?

Because your companions will influence more than just your actions—they will affect the state of your heart and how close you are to Allah. Choose wisely, for their impact will be lasting.

It's easy to get caught up in the hustle and bustle of life and be surrounded by people who are more concerned with worldly things than spirituality. But even in these moments, you have the power to choose. Allah has given us the ability to seek out good company, find those who will walk the path of faith with us, and build relationships with people who are a source of peace and growth.

Finding the Right Supportive Networks

Finding the right companions is not always easy, but it is one of the most valuable things you can do for your spiritual well-being. So, how do you go about finding the right Muslim networks and companions? Here are a few tips:

Engage in Local Communities:
Look for opportunities to connect with other Muslims in your area. Attend local masjids, join study circles, or participate in community events. Many masjids offer women's groups or youth programs to help you build strong connections with others who share your values and faith.

Use Social Media Wisely:
While social media can sometimes be a source of distraction, it can also be a fantastic tool for finding supportive Muslim networks. Follow Islamic scholars, motivational speakers, and like-minded individuals who remind you of Allah. Engage in online discussions, join Muslim groups, and connect with others who can help you stay grounded in your faith.

Find Like-Minded Individuals:

Look for people who share your goals, values, and intentions in faith. Having friends on your spiritual journey can make a huge difference. These people will encourage you when you're down, remind you when you're straying, and celebrate with you when you grow closer to Allah.

Start Small:

If you are unsure where to begin, start with the people around you. Reach out to family members or friends who are strong in their faith and express your desire to grow closer to Allah. Often, people are more than willing to share their wisdom, and you may find that you have had a deeper connection with someone than you initially thought.

Stay True to Yourself:

While it is important to surround yourself with good company, staying true to yourself is equally important. Do not compromise your values just to fit in with a group. Remember that the best companions encourage you to be your best self, not the ones who push you to do things that go against your values.

The Blessing of Supportive Sisterhood

Hana had always wanted to strengthen her connection with Allah, but staying consistent in her prayers felt like an uphill battle. At first, she was determined—setting alarms, making dua, and reminding herself of the rewards. But as days passed, fatigue settled in, and distractions crept into her routine. Some nights, she was too exhausted to rise for Isha; some mornings, she struggled to fight off sleep for Fajr. The guilt was heavy, yet the discipline seemed just out of reach.

Then, she met Amal. They had known each other for years, but their bond deepened when they both confided in each other about their struggles with prayer. "Let's do this together," Amal said one evening. That small promise changed everything.

They became each other's anchors. If Hana missed a prayer, Amal would gently check in: "Have you prayed, love?" never with judgment, only with warmth. On days when Amal felt overwhelmed, Hana would send her a simple reminder: "Allah is waiting for you."

They started texting before each prayer, sometimes just sending a heart emoji as a silent nudge, other times sharing their personal duas. When one of them struggled, the other would offer words of encouragement, reminding her that Allah sees the effort, even in the moments of weakness.

One particularly difficult night, Hana broke down. She felt like she was failing, like she would never be able to pray with the devotion she longed for. Amal called her immediately. "Do you think Allah only loves those who get it right the first time?" she asked. "No, He loves those who keep coming back."

That night, Hana prayed more sincerely than she had long ago. Not because she had mastered consistency, she finally understood that her struggle was part of the journey.

Over time, prayer became easier, not because the distractions disappeared but because she had someone reminding her of why she started. Their friendship became a lifeline—proof that the right company can keep you steady when your own heart wavers.

Today, Hana and Amal continue to hold each other accountable, not just for prayer but for all aspects of their faith. They have learned that sisterhood in Islam is not just about companionship; it is about lifting each other up, reminding each other of their purpose, and walking the path to Allah together.

The Importance of the Right Company

Ultimately, the companions we choose have the power to shape the direction of our lives. If we surround ourselves with people who constantly remind us of Allah and encourage us to seek knowledge and practice our faith, we will naturally be inclined to do the same. But if we surround ourselves with those who distract us from our purpose, we risk losing sight of what truly matters.

The Prophet peace be upon him also said:

> *"The example of a good companion and a bad companion is like that of the one who sells perfume and blows the bellows. As for the*

> *one who sells perfume, he may give you*
> *some, you may buy from him, or you may*
> *smell his fragrance. But as for the one who*
> *blows the bellows, he may burn your clothes,*
> *or you may smell a foul odour." (Sahih al-*
> *Bukhari Hadith 5534)*

This hadith perfectly illustrates the impact of the people we keep around us. Like the perfume seller, good company will bring a sweet fragrance into your life—encouraging, lifting, and reminding you of Allah. On the other hand, bad company will leave you with a foul odour—distracting you, pulling you away from your Deen, and leading you toward things that will harm your soul.

The choice is yours. Surround yourself with the right company. Seek out those who will lift you higher and encourage you to grow in your faith. And in doing so, you'll surround yourself with a community that will bring you closer to Allah, one step at a time.

PART FIVE: WALKING STEADILY TOWARD JANNAH

CHAPTER THIRTEEN
CONSISTENT DEEDS.

I used to think (because that's what I was taught) that to be a "good" Muslim, I had to do something grand—spend hours in deep worship, memorise long surahs in one sitting, or give in charity until it hurt. I thought the road to Jannah was paved with extraordinary acts, which felt almost impossible to sustain.

I would hear stories of scholars who prayed all night, righteous people who gave away everything they owned, and those who fasted every other day. And while these stories inspired me, they made me feel like I wasn't doing enough. I wasn't capable of such intense devotion—so where did that leave me? Was my worship too small to matter? Was I failing because I couldn't maintain these enormous acts of ibadah?

But over time, I learned that in Islam, success isn't about doing something huge once and then burning out. It's about the small, consistent actions that slowly shape you into someone who is always connected to Allah. It's not about how much you do in one moment of enthusiasm—it's about whether you keep doing it, even when the excitement fades.

The Prophet peace be upon him said:

> *"The most beloved deeds to Allah are those that are done consistently, even if they are small." (Sahih al-Bukhari, 6464; Sahih Muslim, 782)*

This hadith completely changed my perspective. It showed me that Allah doesn't expect us to be perfect or demand impossible levels of worship. He wants us to keep showing up, to be consistent, and to build a relationship with Him through small but steady acts of devotion.

I realised I didn't have to wait for a "perfect" moment to worship Allah. I didn't need to block out a day to read the Quran or perform endless Rak'ahs of salah in one night. What mattered more was showing up for Allah every day, even in the smallest ways.

A whispered *SubhanAllah* while washing the dishes. A single ayah before bed. A sincere dua in between daily tasks.

Islam was never meant to be overwhelming. In His infinite mercy, Allah made the path to Him simple and accessible. He values our effort, not the size of our deeds.

Once I understood this, worship no longer felt like a heavy obligation—it felt like love. A daily, quiet, persistent effort to stay close to the One who created me.

Small steps, Big Impact

For years, I struggled to read the Quran regularly. I would tell myself, *"Tomorrow, I'll read a whole juz'."* But that tomorrow rarely came. I kept waiting for the perfect moment—a long, uninterrupted stretch of time— but it never seemed to arrive. Because I felt like I had to do something big, I often ended up doing nothing at all.

Then, I decided to change my approach. Instead of waiting for the perfect moment, I started small—just five minutes a day. That was it. Five minutes of reading, even if it was only a few verses. And something amazing happened: it was easy to do because it was so small. And because it was easy, I kept doing it. What started as five minutes slowly became ten, then fifteen, and soon, reading the Quran became a normal part of my day, like brushing my teeth.

That's the power of consistency. It's not about how much you do but whether you keep doing it.

Think about it:

- If you memorised just one ayah a day, you'd have memorised an entire surah by the end of the year.
- If you give one dollar to charity daily, that's $365 of Sadaqah in a year.
- If you made dua for just one minute after each prayer, that's over 1,800 minutes of talking to Allah in a year.

Small actions, done regularly, create real transformation.

A Detour to Jannah

Every big achievement starts with a small step. Every oak tree begins as a tiny seed. Every "overnight success" is usually years in the making.

Allah says:

> *"And whoever brings a good deed—it will be multiplied tenfold." (Surah Al-An'am 6:160)*

Your five minutes of reading Quran? Allah counts them as fifty. Your $1 of sadaqah? He returns it as Ten.

Your whispered dua? He treasures it in the unseen.

So, stop waiting for the perfect moment or the grand gesture. Start small. Trust that Allah will turn your tiny efforts into something greater than you could imagine.

Building Lifelong Habits of Worship

If you're like me, you've probably experienced bursts of motivation—during Ramadan, after a moving khutbah, or when going through something difficult. But motivation fades. Life gets busy. And if we only rely on feeling inspired, we'll never be consistent.

So, how do we build habits of worship that last?

Start Small and Make It Easy

Don't overwhelm yourself. Pick **one small act** and stick with it. If all your sunnah prayers feel overwhelming, start with just **two extra rak'ah**. If reading a whole page of the

Quran seems hard, read **just one verse**. Make it so easy that you can't say no.

Attach Worship to Something You Already Do

One of the best ways to make worship consistent is to tie it to something you **already** do daily.

- After brushing your teeth in the morning? Say *SubhanAllah wa bihamdihi* 100 times.
- Before checking your phone after Fajr? Read just **one ayah** of the Quran.
- While driving or cooking? Listen to an Islamic lecture or play Quran recitation.

When worship becomes part of your **routine**, it's much easier to maintain.

Don't Underestimate the Power of Dhikr

One of the easiest yet most powerful acts of worship is **Dhikr**—the remembrance of Allah. You don't need extra time, a special place, or even a big effort. You can do it while walking, cleaning, or lying in bed.

The Prophet peace be upon him said:

> *"Shall I tell you about a deed that is easy on the tongue, but heavy on the scale?"*

> *Then he said:*

> *"SubhanAllah wa bihamdihi, SubhanAllah al-'Azim."*

> *(Sahih al-Bukhari, 6406; Sahih Muslim,*

191

2694)

These words take **seconds** to say, yet they are beloved by Allah and carry immense rewards.

Focus on Progress, Not Perfection

There will be days when you slip up. You might forget. You might miss a prayer. You might go weeks without opening the Quran. And that's okay. What matters is that you **start again**. Don't let one missed day turn into a missed week. Don't let guilt stop you from trying again.

Allah doesn't expect perfection—He loves effort.

The Secret to True Success

At the end of the day, we all want success. We chase it in our careers, in our relationships, and in our personal goals. We strive for recognition, stability, and a sense of achievement. We tell ourselves, *If I just get this job, if I just reach this milestone, if I just fix this part of my life— then I'll feel fulfilled.*

But real success isn't found in wealth or status. It's not how many people admire us or how much we own. True success is standing before Allah on the Day of Judgment and knowing that we tried despite our flaws and weaknesses. Despite our struggles, we kept coming back. In the midst of our imperfections, we never stopped seeking Him.

The Prophet peace be upon him said:

"Be steadfast and strive for perfection, but

> *know that you will never be able to do*
> *everything. The most beloved deeds to Allah*
> *are those done consistently, even if they are*
> *small." (Sunan Ibn Majah, 4240)*

This hadith reminds us of something profound: Allah does not expect perfection from us. He knows we will fall short. He knows we will have days where we struggle, our ibadah feels weak, and we feel distant. But what truly matters is that we keep going. That we never give up on our connection with Him.

So don't wait for motivation. Don't wait for the perfect moment. Start today. Start small. Be consistent.

Pray that extra two rak'ahs, even if your heart feels distracted. Whisper *Astaghfirullah* in your moments of frustration. Read just one ayah, even if you don't have the energy for more. These small acts, repeated day after day, shape your heart in ways you can't imagine.

Because in the end, it won't be the one-time grand gestures that matter most. It will be the daily, quiet, sincere efforts—the simple *Alhamdulillah* in hardship, the whispered *Astaghfirullah* in moments of weakness, the single verse read before bed, the small dua made while waiting at a traffic light.

And those small deeds, done with sincerity, will carry us to Jannah. Because true success is not found in how much we accomplish but in how consistently we return to Allah.

CHAPTER FOURTEEN
FACING FUTURE DETOURS
WITH RESILIENCE

Life is not a straight path—it's a winding road with peaks, valleys, and unexpected turns. When you think you've found your footing, another detour appears. Plans unravel, people let you down, and trials emerge out of nowhere, leaving you breathless, wondering how you'll ever move forward.

We have all been there.

In those moments, it's easy to feel lost. It's easy to ask, *Why me? Why now? Why this?* But here's the truth: detours are not punishments but invitations. They are moments that shape, refine, and guide us back to Allah—if we let them. Every difficulty you face is not meant to break you but to awaken something within you. A strength you didn't know you had. A patience you hadn't yet nurtured. A reliance on Allah that deepens with every hardship.

This chapter is your toolkit for navigating life's challenges without losing faith. Because hardship is inevitable, how you respond to it defines you. Whether it's a personal loss that shatters your heart, a professional setback that shakes your confidence, or a spiritual low that makes you feel distant from Allah, you'll learn how to face it with resilience, patience, and unwavering trust in His plan.

You'll learn how to hold onto hope when everything seems hopeless. How to find light when you're surrounded by darkness. How to remind your heart that no matter how stormy life gets, you are never alone—because the One who created you is always near.

So as you move forward, remember this: You don't need to have all the answers. You don't need to be perfect. You just need to keep going. Keep making dua, even when you feel unheard. Keep saying *Alhamdulillah*, even when gratitude feels difficult. Keep returning to Allah, even when you feel unworthy.

Because the road ahead will always have twists and turns. But if your heart is anchored in Him, you will never truly be lost. Every detour, every delay, and every hardship carries a lesson, a pearl of wisdom, and a sign that you are exactly where you need to be. And when you walk with Allah, even the most uncertain path leads to something greater than you ever imagined.

The Nature of Detours: Why They Keep Coming

Allah says:

> *"We will surely test you with something of fear and hunger and loss... But give good*

> *tidings to the patient." (Surah Al- Baraqah 2:155)*

Detours are not signs of failure—they are challenges meant to shape us. They serve as reminders that this world is temporary, and how we rise in the face of difficulty reveals our true resilience.

Key Truths About Detours:

- **They Are Inevitable:** No one is exempt from trials. Even the Prophets faced immense challenges.
- **They Are Temporary:** No storm lasts forever. Allah promises ease after hardship: *"Indeed, with hardship comes ease."* (Surah Ash-Sharh 94:6)
- **They Are Opportunities:** Every detour is a chance to grow closer to Allah and discover new strengths within yourself.

Building Resilience: Practical Tools for Future Challenges

Life will test you. It will throw unexpected challenges your way—loss, disappointment, uncertainty. But resilience is not about avoiding hardships; it's about how you rise after them. It's about how you hold onto faith when everything feels like it's falling apart.

And at the heart of resilience is *sabr*—patience.

Patience is not passive endurance—it's *active* trust in Allah's timing. It's not just gritting your teeth and waiting for the storm to pass; it's standing firm in the storm, knowing that Allah is guiding you through it.

The Prophet peace be upon him said:

> *"How wonderful is the affair of the*
> *believer! His affair is all good, and this is*
> *only for the believer. If something good*
> *happens, he is grateful, and that is good*
> *for him. If something bad happens, he is*
> *patient, and that is good for him."*
> *(Muslim, Hadith 2999)*

This means that no matter what happens—whether life brings blessings or trials—you are always able to gain *khayr* (goodness). The key is *sabr.*

How To Cultivate Sabr:

Reframe the Trial: Instead of asking, *"Why me?"* ask, *"What is Allah teaching me here?"* Every difficulty carries a lesson. Maybe it's a reminder to return to Allah, a chance to grow in strength, or an opportunity to develop gratitude for the things we once took for granted.

Turn to Dua: The Prophet peace be upon him taught us a beautiful supplication for moments of struggle:

> *"O Allah, I seek refuge in You from grief and*
> *sadness, from weakness and laziness, from*
> *miserliness and cowardice, from being*
> *overcome by debt and overpowered by men."*
> *(Bukhari, Hadith 6369)*

197

Dua is not just about asking for relief; it's about surrendering your worries to the One who holds all solutions.

Celebrate Small Wins: Patience isn't built overnight—it's strengthened one small moment at a time. When you resist the urge to complain, choose to trust Allah even when you don't understand, and make even a tiny step forward despite your struggles—*that* is patience in action. Acknowledge your progress.

Story of Sabr:

Samira had built her career with dedication and hard work, but when the pandemic hit, she lost her job. At first, she felt like her world had collapsed. She had bills to pay, responsibilities to manage, and the crushing fear of uncertainty.

But instead of sinking into despair, she decided to shift her mindset. *"Maybe this is a redirection, not a rejection,"* she told herself. She used the time to learn new skills, deepen her Islamic knowledge, and reconnect with Allah.

Months later, she found a job that was *even better* than the one she lost—one that aligned with her values and gave her purpose.

"Allah didn't just give me a new job," she said. *"He gave me a new purpose."*

And this is the essence of *sabr*—trusting that even in the waiting and hardship, Allah is preparing something better for you.

Reliance on Allah (Tawakkul): Letting Go of Control

There's a delicate balance between effort and trust. We often believe that if we plan, work hard, and control every detail, things will go exactly as we want. But life doesn't work that way. Sometimes, despite our best efforts, things fall apart. Doors close. Plans unravel. And in those moments, we feel powerless.

But here's the truth: we were never in control to begin with.

Tawakkul is not about giving up—it's about doing your best while trusting Allah's plan, even when it doesn't align with your expectations. It's about surrendering the illusion of control and finding peace in the knowledge that the One who created you knows exactly what is best for you.

The Prophet peace be upon him said:

> *"If you were to rely upon Allah with the reliance He is due, He would provide for you just as He provides for the birds. They go out in the morning with empty stomachs and return full." (Tirmidhi, Hadith 2344)*

Think about that. The birds don't sit in their nests waiting for food to drop from the sky. They *go out*, they *search*, they *do their part*—but they don't stress over where the next meal will come from. That's *tawakkul*.

How to Practice Tawakkul:

Do Your Best, Then Let Go: Work hard, make the effort,

and take the steps—but remember that the results are in Allah's hands. Your job is to plant the seed; the outcome is His.

Repeat This Dua: "Hasbunallahu wa ni'mal wakeel" *(Allah is sufficient for us, and He is the best Disposer of affairs.)* (Surah At-Tawbah 9:129).

This powerful dua reminds us that Allah is enough no matter how uncertain life feels. Say it when you feel anxious, don't know what to do next, or need reassurance that you're not alone.

Surrender the 'How ': You don't have to figure everything out. You don't have to have all the answers. Sometimes, the doors you're knocking on aren't opening because Allah has a *better* one waiting for you. Your job is to trust that His plan is always greater than your expectations.

Story of Tawakkul

Amira and her husband had been trying to have a child for years. She had done everything she could—medical treatments, lifestyle changes, endless duas. Each month, she hoped for good news, only to face disappointment again and again. She watched as friends announced their pregnancies, and though she was happy for them, her heart ached.

One day, after another negative test, she put her forehead down in sujood and poured her heart out to Allah. *"Ya Allah, I don't understand why this is happening, but I trust You. I trust You know what's best for me, even when I don't."*

A Detour to Jannah

That moment changed everything. Instead of focusing on what she didn't have, she focused on deepening her connection with Allah. She found peace in knowing that whatever was written for her—whether motherhood or another path—was already planned with wisdom and love.

Years later, she and her husband welcomed a child into their lives—not in the way they had expected, but through fostering. At that moment, she realised that *Allah's plan was more beautiful than anything she had ever imagined.*

Tawakkul doesn't mean you won't feel pain. It doesn't mean you won't struggle. But it does mean that, no matter what happens, you trust Allah is leading you to what is *best* for you—even if you can't see it yet.

The Cyclical Nature of Spiritual Growth

We often think of spiritual growth as a straight path—one where we keep moving forward, getting stronger, and never looking back. But in reality, faith is not linear. It ebbs and flows. It has peaks and valleys. Some days, our hearts feel light and connected to Allah. Other days, we struggle to find that connection at all.

Faith is a journey; like the natural world, it moves in seasons. Just as the earth transitions from spring to summer, autumn to winter, our Iman (faith) follows a similar cycle. Recognising where you are and embracing each season's lessons is key.

A Detour to Jannah

The Four Seasons of Iman

Spring (Renewal):

This is when your heart feels awakened—when a reminder touches your soul when you feel inspired to improve when you return to the Quran after being distant. It's a season of growth, clarity, and joy. You feel eager to pray, motivated to seek knowledge, and excited to deepen your relationship with Allah.

Embrace it by:

O *Setting new spiritual goals*

O *Making dua for steadfastness*

O *Strengthening good habits*

Summer (Strength):

This is the time when faith feels easy. You're consistent in your salah, your duas feel powerful, and you carry a sense of certainty in your heart. It's a season of spiritual abundance, where you feel close to Allah and find joy in worship.

Embrace it by:

O *Using this time to store 'spiritual provisions' for harder days.*

O *Helping others who may be struggling.*

O *Deepening your understanding of Islam.*

Autumn (Release):

A Detour to Jannah

This is a season of transition. Maybe you've faced a personal loss, gone through a major life change, or realised you need to let go of certain habits or attachments. It's a time of reflection, where you're shedding old layers of yourself to make room for growth.

Embrace it by:

- Letting go of what no longer serves your faith
- Trusting that change, even when difficult, is necessary for growth.
- Seeking Allah's guidance in times of uncertainty

Winter (Rest):

This is the hardest season—the time when faith feels distant, worship feels heavy, doubts creep in, and you wonder if you'll ever feel spiritually strong again. But as winter is when trees appear barren while their roots grow deep underground, your struggles in this season are not wasted. Your heart still holds onto Allah even when you don't feel it.

Embrace it by:

- Hold onto small acts of worship, even if they feel difficult. Remember that Iman is not always about 'feeling' close to Allah but staying committed despite the distance.

- Trusting that, just like winter, this too shall pass

.

Reflection exercise:

What season are you in right now? How can you embrace its lessons?

In spring or summer, nurture your faith and build strong habits. If you're in autumn or winter, be gentle with yourself and trust that this phase has a purpose. No season lasts forever, and Allah is always near no matter where you are.

And the best part? Just like the earth finds its way back to spring, your heart will find its way back to Him.

Preparing For Future Detours: A Resilience Plan

Life will always have unexpected twists and turns, no matter how much we plan. The loss of a loved one, a sudden health challenge, a shift in our faith, or a personal failure—these are the detours we never see coming. But while we can't always control what happens to us, we can prepare our hearts, minds, and souls to navigate these challenges with strength and trust in Allah.

This resilience plan is your spiritual emergency kit—a way to build a strong foundation before hardship strikes so that you're not left searching for direction when it does.

Build a Strong Foundation

Just like a house needs a solid base to withstand storms,

your faith needs a foundation to help you stay grounded in difficult times. These daily habits will strengthen your connection with Allah and prepare you for whatever lies ahead.

Daily Worship: Salah, Quran, and dhikr are your anchors. They are the daily check-ins that keep your heart tied to Allah, even when everything else feels unsteady. Make them non-negotiable.

Community: Surround yourself with people who uplift and inspire you. A strong support system—friends who remind you of Allah, family members who encourage you, a local masjid or online group—can make all the difference in times of hardship.

Self-Care: Your body and mind are an **amanah** (trust) from Allah. Take care of them. Eat well, rest when needed, and allow time to heal when life overwhelms you. A healthy mind and body will help you navigate life's detours with clarity and patience.

Develop a Crisis Toolkit: Just as we keep first-aid kits for physical emergencies, we need a spiritual and emotional toolkit for life's inevitable hardships. Here are three essential tools to prepare before you need them.

Emergency Dua List: Write down specific duas for different struggles—one for anxiety, one for loss, one for doubt. When your heart feels heavy and words fail you, this list will remind you of the duas that can lift you up. The Prophet peace be upon him often turned to dua in difficult moments, and we can do the same.

Gratitude Journal: Hard times often make us focus on what's missing. A gratitude journal shifts that focus. Write down three things you're grateful for every day, even if they're small—like the warmth of the sun, a kind word from a friend, or the simple ability to breathe. Gratitude softens hardships.

Support System: Know who you can turn to when you need encouragement. A close friend, a mentor, an imam, or even a therapist—having someone to talk to can remind you that you're not alone and that Allah often sends help through people.

Embrace the Process

Resilience isn't about having all the answers—it's about learning to move forward, even when the path is unclear.

Accept Imperfection: You don't have to have it all figured out. Growth is messy. Healing takes time. Spiritual dips are normal. What matters is that you keep turning back to Allah, no matter how many times you fall.

Celebrate Progress: Every step forward is a victory, no matter how small. One extra prayer, one more page of Quran, one moment of patience when you could have reacted with anger—all of it counts. Acknowledge your efforts and keep going.

Trust Allah's Timing: Sometimes, we don't understand why things happen the way they do. But Allah does. Trust that His plan is always wiser, kinder, and better than anything we could have written for ourselves.

Remember: Hardships will come, but so will ease. There will be moments of darkness but also moments of light. The key is to prepare yourself before the storm arrives so that when it does, you have the tools to hold onto Allah—and never let go.

Lessons from Those Who Endured

In times of difficulty, we often feel isolated, as though our struggles are unique to us. However, the beauty of our faith is that we are never truly alone. Through the stories of others who have endured hardship, we can find lessons that strengthen our own resolve and remind us that Allah's wisdom is always present, even in our darkest moments. Here are three stories of resilience—individuals who faced immense challenges and emerged stronger through faith and perseverance.

The Mother Who Lost Her Son

Amina was a mother like any other, filled with love and care for her child, her heart entirely devoted to him. But when her son suddenly passed away, she felt like her world crumbled beneath her. The pain was unbearable, and she couldn't understand how such a tragedy could happen.

For weeks, Amina was consumed with grief. She questioned everything, from the fairness of life to the very existence of her purpose. But when she turned to Allah in the quiet moments, she began to realise something profound. "I realised my son was never mine to keep," she reflected. "He was always Allah's. And one day, I'll see him again."

This thought comforted her—her son had returned to the Creator who gave him life in the first place. Her faith in Allah's plan grew, and she found solace in her belief that all things, both joyous and painful, are in Allah's hands. Amina understood the true meaning of *sabr* (patience) through her grief and how it brings peace even in the face of heartbreaking loss.

Amina's story teaches us that while loss is a part of life, our attachment to Allah should be our deepest connection. With faith and trust, we can heal even the deepest wounds.

The Sister Who Found Resilience After Losing Her Home

Sarah's life took a drastic turn when a devastating fire destroyed her home. She was left with nothing but the clothes on her back and the memories of a life she once knew. In the days following the fire, Sarah experienced profound grief and loss. But amidst the overwhelming sadness, she found a quiet strength rising within her.

She shared, "*It felt like the world was crumbling, but I realised that the material things I lost were never mine. They were blessings from Allah, entrusted to me for a time.*

What I have now, in my heart, is what truly matters."

Sarah's perspective shifted in those moments. She realised that her faith and family were her true treasures, and while she had lost her physical home, her connection to Allah was unshakable. Every day, she made it a point to express gratitude for what remained and focused on rebuilding her life with resilience. *"I can't bring back what was lost, but I can work to create something beautiful with Allah's help,"* she said.

Her journey of rebuilding wasn't just about physical possessions. It became a spiritual renewal. She turned to Allah in dua for guidance and strength, trusting He would provide for her needs in ways she couldn't foresee. Sarah soon became a volunteer at a local organisation, helping other families who had faced similar tragedies. *"Through helping others, I found purpose and peace,"* she shared.

Sarah's story teaches us that there is a way forward, even when we face loss. It reminds us that while things may be taken from us, our faith and connection to Allah are the true anchors that keep us steady. Resilience isn't just about recovering what's lost—it's about trusting in Allah's plan and moving forward, no matter the circumstances.

The Sister Who Found Strength Through Her Struggles with Anxiety

Mariam had always been a vibrant and confident woman. But as she entered her thirties, anxiety crept into her life, a silent yet overwhelming force. She found herself struggling with constant worry, even in the most mundane situations. Her mind became a battlefield, and for a while, she felt disconnected from herself, her faith, and the world around her.

"I couldn't understand why I felt this way," Mariam shared. *"I kept asking myself, 'Why am I so anxious all the time? What's wrong with me?'"*

But through the dark days, Mariam's relationship with Allah became her anchor. She began to turn to Him in moments of fear, seeking comfort through prayer and quiet reflection. Slowly, she realised that her anxiety didn't make her weak— it was an opportunity for growth.

Mariam started to embrace her struggles as part of her personal journey. She learned to lean into the discomfort, trusting that Allah's wisdom was greater than her fear. *"I learned that it's okay to not have all the answers,"* she said. *"My anxiety isn't a punishment; it's a reminder that I need to surrender to Allah's plan and trust that He knows what's best for me."*

Mariam also sought professional help and began incorporating healthy practices into her routine as part of her healing process. She focused on her mental well-being, but always with the understanding that ultimate healing and peace come from Allah. She found solace in small moments—reading the Quran, saying dua, and journaling her thoughts.

Now, Mariam helps others who are struggling with anxiety, using her own experiences to show them that they are not alone. *"It's not about 'fixing' everything,"* she said. *"It's about learning to trust Allah's timing, being patient with yourself, and knowing that peace will come in its own time."*

Her story teaches us that the struggles we face, whether mental or emotional, can be catalysts for spiritual growth. Even in our lowest moments, there's an opportunity to reconnect with Allah and embrace the lessons our struggles offer. True strength comes not from avoiding difficulties but from trusting Allah through them.

Lessons: Each of these stories teaches us that resilience is not about avoiding hardship but how we respond to it. Whether it's grief, loss, illness, or any other struggle, these individuals showed us that we can overcome even the toughest challenges with faith, trust in Allah's wisdom, and perseverance.

Their resilience is not about never falling but rising each time we do, with the knowledge that every trial is a chance to grow closer to Allah. In the end, our connection to Him and our reliance on His mercy give us the strength to endure whatever life throws our way.

The Duas for Resilience

For Patience:"Ya Allah, grant me patience in the face of trials. Let me see Your wisdom in every challenge."
For Trust:"Ya Wakil (The Trustee), I place my trust in You.

Guide me through this storm and bring me to safety."

For Strength:"Ya Muqallib al-Quloob (The Turner of Hearts), keep my heart firm on Your deen, no matter what comes my way."

The Journey Continues

Detours are not the end of the road—they are part of the journey. They remind us that this life is temporary and that our true destination is with Allah.

The Resilience Pledge

Write a promise to yourself:
"I will face future challenges with patience, trust, and faith."

"I will remember that every detour is an opportunity to grow closer to Allah."

Seal it with a dua:

"Ya Allah, help me navigate the road ahead with courage and resilience. Amen

---

CHAPTER FIFTEEN
JANNAH AWAITS

In the hustle and bustle of life, it's easy to become consumed by this world's glittering marketplace—a cacophony of desires where temporary pleasures shout louder than eternal truths. We chase after wealth like children chasing fireflies, mistaking their fleeting glow for the sun. We clamber for status, building towers of ego that crumble under the weight of a single setback. We nestle into comfort, mistaking padded routines for purpose as if life were a waiting room rather than a journey toward the Divine. These distractions are not inherently evil, but they are illusions— mirage pools in a desert that leave us thirstier the more we drink.
The Prophet peace upon him warned:

> *"By Allah, it is not poverty that I fear for you,*
> *but rather that worldly wealth will be*
> *bestowed upon you as it was bestowed upon*
> *those before you, and you will compete for it*
> *as they competed, and it will destroy you as*
> *it destroyed them" (Bukhari Hadith 3158).*

Yet Allah, in His wisdom, does not ask us to abandon the world—only to see it for what it is: a test, a tool, and a fleeting corridor leading to the true destination. The *real* treasure—radiant, eternal, and untainted by decay—lies beyond the veil of this life: **Jannah**. It is not merely a reward for good deeds; it is the ultimate expression of Allah's mercy, a love letter written in rivers of milk and honey, where every promise of comfort in this world is a shadow compared to its reality.

Jannah: The Eternal Oasis

Imagine a realm where:

- **Time collapses**: A single moment there outshines a thousand lifetimes here (Surah Al-Hajj 22:47).
- **Pain dissolves**: Every tear shed in Dunya is replaced with profound joy; *"no soul has ever conceived"* its fullness (Surah As-Sajda 32:17).
- **Longing ceases**: The heart's restless search for belonging finds its home in the presence of the Most Merciful.

Allah (SWT) describes Jannah as a place where:

> *"They will have whatever they wish, and with Us is even more" (Surah Qaf 50:35).*

But Jannah is more than gardens and palaces—it is *nearness*. It is sitting with the Prophets, laughing with martyrs, and seeing the Face of Allah, the source of all light and peace. It is the culmination of every "why" whispered in hardship, every act of patience in the dark, every *sajdah* made with trembling hope.

The Illusion of "Enough"

This world's trinkets are designed to leave us wanting. A bigger house demands a bigger lock. More wealth breeds more worry. Status is a ladder with no top rung—climb all day, and you'll only fear the fall. But Jannah's blessings are infinite, *multiplying* with gratitude rather than diminishing:

> *"And whatever you have of favour—it is from Allah" (Surah An-Nahl 16:53).*

A Bedouin once asked the Prophet peace be upon him, "What is the reality of this world?" He replied:

> *"Be in this world as if you were a stranger or a traveller." (Sahih al-Bukhari Hadith 6416)*

A Call to Reorient

This is not a call to abandon the world but to **reclaim your compass**:

Ask daily: *"Is what I'm chasing today worth trading for a moment in Jannah?"*

Invest in eternity: Every dollar given in charity, every word of Quran recited, every act of kindness is a seed planted in the soil of the hereafter.

Replace fear with longing: Don't worship Allah out of terror of hellfire, though heed its warnings, but out of yearning for His presence. As Rabia al-Adawiyya prayed: *"If I worship You for fear of Hell, burn me in Hell. If I worship You for the hope of Paradise, exclude me from it. But if I worship You for You alone, do not withhold Your Eternal Beauty."*

The Beauty Of Jannah: A Glimpse Into Eternity

The Quran and Hadith give us glimpses of Jannah to inspire and remind us of what we strive for. Imagine:

Rivers of pure water, milk, honey, and wine flowing beneath your feet, their taste and purity unlike anything in this world. (Surah Muhammad 47:15)

Gardens of endless shade, where the trees are so vast that riding a horse for a hundred years would not cover their expanse. (Muslim Hadith 345)

Palaces of gold and pearls, where every room is more beautiful than the last and where the believers will reside in comfort and luxury.

The company of the Prophets, the martyrs, and the righteous is where you will meet those you admired and loved in this life and where you will be reunited with your loved ones who shared your faith.

But perhaps the greatest blessing of Jannah is the pleasure of Allah Himself. The Prophet Muhammad (peace be upon him) said:

> *"When the people of Jannah enter Jannah,*
> *Allah will say, 'Do you wish for Me to give*
> *you anything more?' They will say, 'Have*
> *You not made our faces bright? Have You not*
> *admitted us into Jannah and saved us from*
> *the Fire?' Then Allah will remove the veil,*
> *and they will see nothing more beloved than*
> *the sight of their Lord." (Sahih Muslim*
> *Hadith 348)*

This is the ultimate reward—the joy of seeing Allah, the Most Merciful and being in His presence for eternity. It surpasses all worldly pleasures and fulfils the deepest longing of the human soul.

The Path to Jannah: A Journey of Faith and Struggle

While the beauty of Jannah is undeniable, it is not easily attained. It requires effort, sacrifice, and unwavering faith. Allah (SWT) says:

> *"Or do you think that you will enter Paradise*
> *while such [trial] has not yet come to you as*
> *came to those who passed on before you?*
> *They were touched by poverty and hardship*
> *and were shaken until [even their] messenger*
> *and those who believed with him said, 'When*
> *is the help of Allah?' Unquestionably, the*
> *help of Allah is near." (Surah Al-Baqarah*
> *2:214)*

A Detour to Jannah

This life is a test, and Jannah is the reward for those who pass it. The path to Jannah is paved with patience, perseverance, and trust in Allah. It requires us to resist temptations, overcome challenges, and remain steadfast in our worship and good deeds. Every Salah we pray, every Quranic verse we recite, every act of kindness we perform, and every sin we avoid brings us closer to Jannah.

But let's be honest—the journey is not easy. There will be moments of weakness, times when we stumble, and days when the weight of our struggles feels unbearable. In those moments, remember Jannah. Remember that every hardship you endure, every tear you shed, and every sacrifice you make is a step closer to eternal bliss. The Prophet Muhammad (peace be upon him) said:

> *"Jannah is surrounded by hardships, and the Hellfire is surrounded by desires." (Sahih Muslim Hadith 349)*

The path to Jannah may be difficult but worth every struggle. On the other hand, the path to Hell may seem easy and tempting, but it leads to eternal regret. Choose wisely.

A Heartfelt Dua: Turning to Allah for Guidance and Mercy

As we reflect on the beauty of Jannah and the challenges of this life, let us turn to Allah with sincere hearts and ask

Him to guide us, forgive us, and grant us the ultimate success. Here is a heartfelt dua to conclude this chapter:

"O Allah, You are the Most Merciful, the Most Generous. We come to You with hearts full of hope and longing for Jannah. O Allah, make us among those who strive for Your pleasure, remain steadfast in the face of trials, and never lose sight of the eternal reward You have prepared for the righteous.

O Allah, forgive our sins, purify our hearts, and strengthen our faith. Grant us the patience to endure hardships, the wisdom to avoid temptations, and the courage to stay on Your path, no matter how difficult it may seem.

O Allah, we long for Jannah—the home of peace and the righteous abode. We long to see Your face, to be in Your presence, and to experience the joy that no eye has seen, no ear has heard, and no heart has ever imagined.

O Allah, make us among those who enter Jannah without reckoning, are saved from the Fire, and are granted the highest ranks in Paradise.

Ameen."

A Call To Action: Stay On The Path, No Matter The Detours

Dear reader, the journey to Jannah is not a straight path. There will be detours, obstacles, and moments of doubt.

But remember, every step you take in obedience to Allah brings you closer to your ultimate destination. No matter how far you may stray, never lose hope in Allah's mercy. He is the Most Forgiving, the Most Compassionate. Return to Him, seek His forgiveness, and continue striving.

Let Jannah's promise be your motivation. Let its beauty inspire you to be better, to do better, and to never give up. The road may be long, but the reward is eternal. So, stay on the path, no matter the detours. Jannah awaits, and its gates are open for those who never give up.

The journey is yours to take. Will you strive for Jannah?

CONCLUSION
YOUR JOURNEY IS YOURS ALONE

Dear sister or brother, as you stand at the crossroads of your spiritual journey, remember that Allah has crafted your path with divine precision.

The Qur'an affirms:

> *"We have created you into nations and tribes so that you may know one another" (49:13)*

Celebrating diversity in worship and experience. Your journey is a tapestry of trials and triumphs, uniquely tailored to your soul's growth.

The Prophet Muhammad (PBUH) said:

> *"How wonderful is the affair of the believer! His matters are all good... If he is tested with hardship, he is patient, and that is good for him" (Sahih Muslim 2999).*

Your struggles are not random—they are purposeful, designed to draw you closer to the One who knows your heart best.

Sincerity Over Perfection: The Heart of Worship

Allah cherishes your sincere efforts, not flawless execution.

Consider the story of Abu Bakr (RA), who wept despite his unwavering faith, fearing his intentions might not be pure. The Prophet (PBUH) reassured him, *"Your tears are a mercy from Allah"* (Al-Bukhari).

This teaches us that vulnerability is a bridge to divine grace.

Reflect on Surah Al-Zumar 39:53:

> *"Say, 'O My servants who have transgressed against themselves: Despair not of Allah's mercy, for Allah forgives all sins.'"*

Your repentance, like the man finding his camel in the desert, ignites divine joy. Let this truth dissolve shame— your value lies in your *Tawbah* (repentance), not perfection.

Trusting Divine Wisdom: Stories of Resilience

When uncertainty clouds your path, remember Prophet Yaqub (AS), who endured decades of separation from his son Yusuf (AS), yet never ceased trusting Allah. His eventual reunion was a testament to divine timing:

> *"Indeed, my Lord is Subtle in what He*
> *wills" (12:100).*

Similarly, Hajar (AS)'s desperate run between Safa and Marwah underlines *Tawakkul* (trust). Though alone in the desert, her faith summoned the miracle of Zamzam.

Allah's promise in Surah At-Talaq 65:3:

> *"And whoever relies upon Allah—He is*
> *sufficient for them,"*

Is a lifeline. Trust that your "detours" are divine redirects, guiding you where you need to be.

Hope Anchored in Mercy

Allah's mercy eclipses all human frailty. The Prophet (PBUH) shared,

"Allah says, 'My mercy prevails over My wrath'" (Sahih Bukhari 7422).

Each dawn is a rebirth—a theme echoed in Surah An-Nahl 16:97:

> *"Whoever does righteousness, whether male*
> *or female, while believing—We will surely*
> *grant them a good life."*

Embrace this hope: your "darkest night" is a prelude to dawn. When despair whispers, recite the dua of Yunus (AS):

> *"La ilaha illa Anta, Subhanaka! Inni kuntu minaz-zalimin" (None has the right to be worshipped but You; I have been among the wrongdoers) (21:87).*

This invocation rescued him from the belly of a fish; let it anchor you in storms.

Empowerment Through Community and Solitude

While your journey is personal, you are never isolated. The Qur'an describes believers as *"brothers"* (49:10), bound by mutual support. Yet, balance communal ties with solitary reflection. The Prophet (PBUH) retreated to Cave Hira for contemplation before revelation. Carve moments of K*halwa* (solitude) to converse with Allah. In gatherings, seek those who mirror Surah Al-Asr 103:3:

> *"Those who enjoin truth and patience."*

If surrounded by negativity, remember the wisdom of Luqman:

> *"Do not turn your cheek in scorn toward people" (31:18)—*

Walk away with grace, protecting your peace.

A Du'a for the Journey

"O Allah, transform my doubts into certainty, my fears into faith, and my silence into supplications. Let my heart find solace in Your remembrance, my steps strength in Your plan, and my soul peace in Your promise. When I falter, remind me that Your mercy outruns my sins. When I feel alone, wrap me in the love of those who reflect Your light. And when I meet You, let my story be a testament to Your endless grace. Ameen."

Final Steps Forward

Your journey is a mosaic of divine love—every tear, prayer, and stumble a piece of the masterpiece. As you turn the page, carry this truth: Jannah's gates await not the perfect, but the persevering. Walk with courage, for Allah walks with you. *"And the Hereafter is better for you than the first [life]"* (93:4). Your new beginning starts now, hand in hand with the Most Merciful.

ACKNOWLEDGMENT

All praise is due to Allah, the Most Merciful, the Most Kind. Without His guidance, strength, and endless mercy, this book would not have been possible. He is the One who lights the path for those who seek Him, mends hearts that have wandered, and welcomes every soul that turns back in repentance. I am deeply grateful for the inspiration, clarity, and perseverance He has granted me throughout this journey.

To my beloved Prophet Muhammad peace be upon him, whose life and teachings serve as the ultimate guide to truth, may endless peace and blessings be upon him.

I extend my heartfelt gratitude to my family, whose unwavering support and love have carried me through the highs and lows of this journey. To my husband and children—you are my greatest blessings, and your patience and encouragement mean more than words can express.

To my teachers, mentors, and those who have guided me in my pursuit of knowledge—whether you know it or not—thank you for your wisdom and for reminding me that seeking Ilm is a lifelong journey.

To my readers, whether you are returning to the Deen or strengthening your faith, I pray that this book serves as a source of light and hope for you. May Allah make it a means of drawing us closer to Him, and may He accept it as a small effort in the path of His pleasure.

Finally, to anyone who has made dua for me, supported me, or encouraged me in any way—Jazakum Allahu khayran. May Allah bless you abundantly and grant us all the ability to remain steadfast on the path to Jannah.

With love and prayers
See you in Jannah (Insha-Allah)

Your Sister, Hajer

And my success is not but through Allah. – [Surah Hud11:88]

ABOUT THE AUTHOR

Hajer Jemai is a dedicated researcher, educator, and writer passionate about faith, personal growth, and culturally and religiously sensitive healthcare.
With a background in psychology and public health, she is pursuing a PhD to explore the impact of religious and cultural sensitivity in maternity care on the mental well-being of Muslim women in Australia.

Beyond academia, she is an educator, an advocate for community well-being, and a devoted mother who believes in the transformative power of knowledge and faith. Her writing reflects her deep commitment to guiding others toward spiritual fulfilment, resilience, and a meaningful connection with Allah.
In A Detour to Jannah, she shares heartfelt reflections, practical advice, and faith-centred wisdom to help readers navigate the challenges of modern life while staying grounded in their Deen.

When she's not writing or researching, she enjoys playing with her children, exploring nature, and working on faith-based initiatives that empower and uplift others.

www.ingramcontent.com/pod-product-compliance
Lightning Source LLC
Chambersburg PA
CBHW031938090426

42811CB00002B/223